D0285913

Also by Steven A. Emerson

The Fall of Pan Am 103 (co-authored with Brian Duffy)
*Secret Warriors: Inside the Covert Military Operations
of the Reagan Era*
American House of Saud: The Secret Petrodollar Connection

TERRORIST

TERRORIST

The Inside Story of the Highest-Ranking Iraqi Terrorist Ever to Defect to the West

Steven A. Emerson
and Cristina Del Sesto

VILLARD BOOKS
New York
1991

Acknowledgments

There are many people who agreed to be interviewed for this book—some on the record, some off. The sensitive nature of part of the material provided to me precludes me from thanking various people by name—but their assistance will always be deeply appreciated. Most of the officials interviewed in this book represented intelligence and law-enforcement agencies of the U.S. government, although I also interviewed intelligence and counterterrorist officials based out of Switzerland, Israel, Germany, Greece, France, Great Britain, and Egypt.

Those who spoke to me on the record are cited in these pages and I very much appreciate the time they gave me.

The technical details surrounding Abu Ibrahim's bombs comes largely from two sources: an unpublished paper by former FBI explosives expert Denny Kline, who did not provide the paper to me, but did confirm that he wrote it and also shared some human-interest details about his experiences in the FBI; and Billy Vincent, formerly of the Federal Aviation Administration, who has been one of the leading crusaders for tightened anti-terrorism airline security. Internal FBI and CIA documents were provided to me by government officials who will have to remain nameless, but whose interest was motivated by their desire to see the behind-the-scenes nature of the government's fight against terrorism revealed.

I wish to thank the many people who made this book possible. First and foremost is Cristina Del Sesto, who

ACKNOWLEDGMENTS

drafted much of the material dealing with Adnan's personal life. Cristina's gifted feature writing is matched only by her wonderful sense of humor.

I am forever in debt to my agent, Esther Newberg, of ICM, who is the embodiment of every author's ideal book agent. Esther's support, encouragement, and belief in this project is the only reason this book was possible.

Brian Duffy's editorial suggestions proved invaluable.

I am also indebted to Helena Smith, who works for *The Guardian* in Athens, and provided some of the background material on Mohammed Rashid.

I wish to express my deepest appreciation to Pam Hill and John Lane of CNN's Special Assignment, for their encouragement—and for their patience with and understanding of my erratic work schedule. Pam Hill towers above everyone else in broadcast journalism—and I am grateful for the opportunity she has provided me to enter the field.

Also at CNN, I want to express my gratitude for last-minute help to Peter Bergen, an unusually talented producer, who surely will become known as one of the best producers in the country. David Lewis, another CNN colleague, provided constant encouragement through his wicked sense of humor. His uncanny ability to call me at the worst possible moments will never be forgotten.

I would like to thank a friend who I consider to be one of the most dynamic magazine editors in the country, Peter Bloch of *Penthouse* magazine, where portions of Adnan's story first appeared.

In the end, the people who made this happen were Peter Gethers and his crew at Villard Books, who worked around the clock to get this project completed. Peter has an editor's touch that is truly magical. Amy Edelman's copy editing of the manuscript was magnificent; her changes and suggestions improved the manuscript immeasurably. Pat Follert and Maureen McMahon worked tirelessly in the publicity department.

Last but not least, I wish to thank Adnan Awad, who I believe has made one of the most important individual contributions to American national security in the past decade. I fervently hope that one day soon he will get what is long overdue him—American citizenship and a U.S. passport.

Contents

Prologue

I met Adnan at a deli last November.

I had spoken to a man three weeks earlier who wouldn't identify himself on the telephone. He spoke with an Arabic accent and told me he had an incredible story to tell.

As a reporter I've been on the receiving end of many telephone calls from people with "incredible stories" who simply want to talk to someone, so I was suspicious.

Still, there was something about the sincerity of this man, a certain innocence about him, that made me instinctively believe he was not a con artist.

His story unraveled and, while I wanted to believe him, it all seemed too spectacular. A former Iraqi terrorist living in the United States? This was something I had never heard of—not even in fiction. It did not seem plausible.

I agreed then to meet Adnan in person. Through the window of the deli, I saw a tall, olive-skinned man, a jacket casually slung over his shoulder. His silver hair—or what was left of it—was pulled back in a small ponytail. With him was a tall, attractive blond woman. I thought they looked more like a couple from Hollywood than from Baghdad.

Adnan graciously introduced himself, apologized for his broken English, and, following some awkward attempts at small talk, immediately launched into a discussion of how much he loved Jerry Lewis movies.

An Iraqi terrorist who liked Jerry Lewis movies sitting in a deli being served by old matronly Jewish waitresses? This was a bit much. Surely I was wasting my time.

But as the man talked, there was no bluster, no bravado, no apparent desire to embellish. He seemed to be telling the truth.

I sat enraptured as Adnan proceeded to tell me his story. By the end of our meeting, I realized I was fascinated and captivated by his yarn. If true, it would prove to be one of the most important stories of the past decade: A man who was inside an Iraqi terrorist gang had defected to the United States and entered the Witness Protection Program, yet for all intents and purposes was being shut up by the government of the very country he was trying to help! If there was anyone who could have provided indisputable evidence that Iraq had continued to support terrorism, it was this eyewitness!

Still, at this point, that's all Adnan's story was—a yarn. I had no way of knowing whether any of it was truthful. I needed to do my own checking. Could I have his last name and Social Security number? I asked. No, he couldn't give me his last name and he didn't have a Social Security number. Ah, I thought to myself, the perfect alibi for a fabricator. Despite that certain something in his mannerisms, in his direct gaze, in his measured responses that was telling me he was in fact telling the truth, when I said good-bye, I had a nagging feeling that I just would not be able to confirm this man's story.

When I returned to Washington, I made several telephone calls to friends of mine at the FBI and CIA. I knew I had to be a bit evasive—I couldn't come right out and tell them that I just met a man purporting to be a former terrorist who was now in the Witness Protection Program. If there was any chance that this man named Adnan was telling the truth, I couldn't afford to reveal the fact that I had spoken to him. Because of the extraordinary security threat he was facing, the government had prohibited him from making *any* contact with the media. When he traveled to another city, the government arranged for federal marshals to escort him and had him travel to several other cities before he was allowed to arrive at his real destination. If this man actually turned out to be legitimate and I had let on that I had spoken to him, it would surely leak back to Adnan's handlers. And if that happened, they would probably shut him down.

In my inquiries to government officials, I asked if they were aware of a former Iraqi terrorist who had defected to the United States. Then I recalled that several years ago, in preparation for a previous book on counterterrorism, I had been told about a "walk-in," someone with connections to a terrorist group who had given himself up in Europe in the mid-1980s. That was about all I knew— and it didn't seem that important to me at the time. After all, the United States has lots of two-bit informants professing inside information on terrorist groups. Most of the time, they are never really connected—they have a friend who is connected, making hearsay a lucrative business, especially with the American counterterrorist and intelligence services.

But now it seemed that the man who called himself

Adnan was the same walk-in. Much to my amazement, the government officials told me that indeed there was a man who had given himself up. They couldn't recall his name offhand but he was a terrorist connected to the Abu Ibrahim group in Iraq, and when he gave himself up, he also surrendered the bomb that he had been instructed to plant. I spoke to several other officials, who affirmed their trust in Adnan and said he was considered to be 100 percent reliable. So reliable, in fact, that he was going to be the chief witness against a Palestinian terrorist held in Greece whose legal status had been at the center of a tug-of-war between Greece and the United States for the last two and a half years.

I began interviewing Adnan. He was, in fact, the first witness for the West to the irrefutable fact that Iraq had institutionalized terrorism into an instrument of Iraqi foreign policy. He was living proof that the Iraqi government, despite claims back in 1982, had never given up terrorism. Yet, six months before Adnan defected, the United States had taken Iraq *off* the list of countries found to be supporting terrorism. In February 1982, the United States had given Iraq a completely clean bill of health. Ever since then, U.S. policy toward Iraq had spiraled out of control, picking up powerful vested interests along the way in U.S. government, business, and academia. This myopic policy toward Iraq reached its height in 1986, when the United States shared aerial reconnaissance photos of Iranian troop formations in an effort to tilt the military balance against Iran in the Iran-Iraq war. Those photos would come back to haunt the United States when Iraq was able to hold on to Kuwait for the first five weeks of the Persian Gulf war despite intense American and allied air bombardment; Iraqi familiarity with American intelligence and satellite capabilities enabled the Iraqis to devise effective ways to hide its Scud missile launchers and other weapons.

From 1982 through August 1, 1990, this "special relationship" with Iraq continued to blossom, despite powerful and incontestable evidence that Iraq remained a country that used terrorism internally and externally to silence critics and murder those with a Western and/or Jewish background.

Of course, the real nature of Iraq and its leader, Saddam Hussein, hit the United States fiercely when Iraq invaded Kuwait on August 2, 1990. Suddenly, Saddam Hussein became a "Hitler" overnight. The media frenzy detailing Iraq's ties to terrorists has not stopped since.

But in point of truth, Saddam Hussein did not become a Hitler overnight, nor did his regime suddenly transform itself into a terrorist-supporting nation. For the past nine years, ever since the United States initiated its pro-Iraq policy in the conflict with Iran—a policy that culminated in the war in the Persian Gulf—Iraq had never stopped supporting terrorism. Ronald Reagan had initiated an alliance with a police state that made East Germany look tame in comparison.

In the end, there is no way of verifying *everything* that has happened to Adnan. But officials of the CIA, FBI, Justice Department, and Pentagon—several of whom have gone on the record in this book—as well as Swiss and Israeli intelligence officials, have independently confirmed the accuracy of much of his story, specifically the details regarding what has happened since he defected. Much of the information he has provided to American intelligence agencies regarding Iraq, Iraqi terrorism, and Iraqi bombs has been also independently confirmed by exhaustive interrogation of captured Iraqi terrorists and informants and documents obtained by Western intelligence and counterterrorist agencies. Perhaps the most profound indicator of the government's trust in Adnan is the Justice Department's use of Adnan as the prime witness against a terrorist now being held in Greece.

For Adnan, there is little relief in knowing that he has been vindicated. He can never go home again. This is his truly remarkable story.

—STEVEN A. EMERSON
Washington, D.C.
March 1991

TERRORIST

1

Growing Up in Palestine

Adnan Awad got cold feet.

It wasn't the first time, either. Twice before, his parents had agreed that he would marry. And as each bride-to-be came of age, he found reasons to go against their wishes.

But on August 31, 1982, it wasn't a bride he was leaving behind. It was a bomb.

As a Palestinian terrorist sent by Abu Ibrahim, one of the most dangerous terrorists in the world, to destroy the Geneva Noga Hilton in Switzerland, Awad's decision not to comply meant a lot more than hurting Ibrahim's feelings.

His disobedience has cost him his family, his business, his four cars, his home, his considerable investments, and . . . even his name.

Even though Abu Ibrahim and his terrorist cronies are believed by American and Israeli intelligence agencies to have put a multimillion-dollar contract on Adnan, concealing his whereabouts and his past by repeatedly changing his name has been the most injurious result of Adnan's actions eight years ago.

3

He says he can survive the pain of missing his family. He can easily sustain himself without the money and grand life-style he'd become accustomed to. He can even live each day under the threat of Ibrahim's revenge. But without the name he was born with, he says, his identity has become obscured. "I've lost myself," he says.

Adnan Awad knew who he was once but he can't keep track of who he is today.

High in the Carmel mountain range overlooking the Mediterranean Sea and the city of Haifa ten miles away, Adnan lived the first years of his life in the village of Ijzim, Palestine. In 1942, the year he was born, Israel did not exist. Palestine was governed by the British under the Mandate, granted to Britain by the League of Nations at the San Remeo Conference in 1920. There was to be full recognition of "the historical connection for the Jewish people with Palestine and . . . the grounds for reconstituting their national home in that country." The Mandate actually covered what is today Jordan and Israel, but in 1921 Great Britain separated the area east of the river Jordan named Transjordan and gave it to the emir Abdullah.

Spurred by rising anti-Semitism in Europe and, eventually, the emergence of Adolf Hitler, Jewish immigration to Palestine continued through the 1920s and 1930s, only to be greeted by growing Palestinian Arab resistance to the prospect of Jews living there and ultimately becoming a majority. By 1933, according to British historian Martin Gilbert, the Jewish population had increased to 400,000, equal to approximately one third of the total Arab population, and there began to be spurts of violence, largely Arab attacks on Jewish civilians and settlements. This finally erupted in a massive and coordinated campaign of violence directed at the Jewish community in 1936. On May 13 of that year, the mufti of Jerusalem declared, in a fiery speech delivered in Haifa, that the "Jews are trying to expel us from our country. They are murdering our sons and burning our houses." Exhorting the Arabs to attack Jews, the mufti incited a four-month series of fatal attacks—bombings, stabbings, lynchings—on Jews throughout Palestine, resulting in the deaths of hundreds of Jews.

In response to the attacks, and in order to protect their communities, the Jews began organizing themselves into militias. This growing civil war between Arab and Jew could not be contained, even as British officials vacillated over how to dispose of the much-contested piece of real estate. As Zionist leaders fought for the right to establish a homeland and Arab leaders demanded that Jews be expelled, the British decided, in 1947, to hand their problem over to the United Nations. On November 29 of that year, the U.N. General Assembly voted to establish two separate states, one for Jews and the other for Arabs, under what became known as the United Nations Partition Plan.

The Jews accepted the decision; the Arabs did not. The entire area erupted in even more violence as Palestinian Arabs, incited by neighboring Arab states, attacked Jews wherever and whenever they could. The Hagannah, the emerging Jewish defense force, responded, as did the Jewish terrorist underground, with reprisals against the Arabs. A full-scale war had exploded.

On May 15, 1948, the Jews proclaimed the independent state of Israel in the area allocated to them under the U.N. Partition Plan. On the same day, five Arab armies—

Egyptian, Transjordanian, Syrian, Iraqi, and Lebanese—
invaded Palestine in an effort to crush the Jewish state.
The Jews were under siege throughout their territory—
their forces nearly overwhelmed by the invading Arab
forces in the north, the Galilee region; the Jerusalem area;
and the Negev, the southern area. But the Hagannah
fought back with a vengeance.

Adnan knew very little of the hatred between Arab and
Jew. "All I knew was my village," he recalled. "I knew
nothing of America, Israel, or Syria."

Ijzim was dominated by olive groves, lemon and orange
orchards, and chickens, which roamed freely about the
sloping land, laying their eggs beneath bushes and neighbors' porches.

"It would take us half a day to walk from the top of the
mountain to the valley," Adnan said. "And all the way
down we would eat the wild fruit that grew there."

Adnan's father was the second richest man in the village. It was at a wedding in a neighboring town by the sea
that he had first seen Adnan's mother, Widad, whose
name means "Love and Chastity" in Arabic. As was the
custom, he went through parental intermediaries to ask
for her hand. Permission was granted and they were married.

Soon Widad was pregnant. Their firstborn was a daughter. No one in particular was impressed.

Two years later, in 1942, Adnan arrived.

Adnan's father owned the only store in the village. It
supplied the people with everything from shoes to meat to
kerosene.

At the time of Adnan's birth his father was hard at

work, but all the young women ran to tell him the news: He had a son.

It is Arab custom to commemorate such an achievement by adding the prefix "abu" to the sire's name. His father would forever more be known as Abu Adnan.

"I remember him telling me the story over and over," Adnan said. "He took a wash bin from his inventory, filled it with candy, and invited the entire village to celebrate."

Adnan's older sister was acutely aware of the deferential treatment.

"My sister was jealous," Adnan said. "I could go out, she couldn't. I could wear shorts in the summer, she had to be covered. My grandmother would always sit me on her lap, but nobody would pay any attention to my sister. She couldn't understand. But even then I knew. I was better."

Adnan was "better" than all of his seven brothers and three sisters. Whatever he did wrong in his village was forgiven. Such early privileges set the foundation for a habit of living on the edge of danger without fear of punishment or retribution.

In 1948, when Adnan was six years old, the sounds of war echoed in the distance. It was the first time Adnan heard anyone mention the word "Jews."

"People said that the 'Jews' were coming to take our homes away and that if you were wearing a ring they would cut your finger off just to get it," he said. "And I thought to myself, 'The Jewish people are something scary.'"

Meanwhile, Abu had to keep his store stocked. He would go on trips for supplies—to faraway places that Adnan couldn't pronounce but imagined going to someday.

One night when his father was on such a trip, Adnan's mother gave Adnan the key to the store and sent him there for food. But when he got there he found the shelves empty.

He quickly returned to his mother and told her the news. He could sense her fury as he stood looking up into her face, which usually radiated with kindness and love. She set about to find out who was responsible for the thievery; Adnan grabbed hold of her dress, clinging tightly as she ran.

The crowd waiting for her outside of the store accused Abu Adnan of being a traitor. "They said he had left and was not coming back," Adnan said. "But this was completely wrong. He was just getting supplies as he normally did."

Later his mother told him, "I wish the Jews had taken all of these supplies rather than a lying cousin making up excuses."

The 1948 war of independence for the Jews was the first Arab-Israeli war. For many rural Arab villages, however, it was a distant conflict. Arab radio broadcasts continued to disseminate false reports of Arab victories over the Jews; at the same time, they reported that Jews were committing the most savage atrocities imaginable—for example, ripping embryos from the stomachs of pregnant Arab women. Arab leaders exhorted Palestinian communities to flee from the marauding Jewish armies, helping the established Arab forces in their efforts to destroy the fledgling Jewish state. Palestinians were promised that once the Arab armies conquered Palestine, the Palestinians could return to their homes. But there was also widespread panic sown by the activities of the underground

Jewish terror networks, known as the Stern Gang and the Irgun. In one of the most savage episodes, hundreds of Arab civilians in the village of Deir Yassin, on the outskirts of Jerusalem, were massacred.

Even in the small village where Adnan lived, insulated as it was from the growing conflict, it was clear the war was getting worse. In preparation, Adnan's mother had the children help her dig a hole underneath the chicken coop, where she buried her treasured belongings. Then she gathered together a bag of flour and some cheese and took her children to meet other families at the home of the richest man in the village. "Some said nobody would bomb his house because he agreed with the Jews," Adnan said.

The next day the Hagannah entered the village. "I remember everybody thinking, 'Now they will rape and kill us,' " Adnan said. His mother smeared her face with dirt and ashes to make herself unattractive. But instead of being tortured, he and his family—along with the rest of their village—were taken to an Israeli army base. There everyone was given challah, the traditional Jewish bread, and marmalade.

Still, the villagers, most of whom had never met a Jew, were distrustful of the Hagannah soldiers. The stories they had heard had been so violent they wondered if the food was poisoned. No one would eat until someone pointed at a mentally retarded teenager. His challah was nearly gone, yet he was still alive.

"Everybody watched him and then we began eating too," Adnan said. He remembers being treated surprisingly well by those he had come to fear. The Hagannah said that the people could stay in the camp or be given a ride to the Jordanian border. More than three quarters of the village decided to leave. Adnan's mother, although worried about her husband, thought it would be best for them to go too.

It was summertime and the river was low. Adnan remembers that the water was up to his knees and felt good as it swirled around him.

His mother was juggling two of the younger children, one in her arm and the other on her hip, and so she gave Adnan a sack of flour to carry. But after a while he got tired and discarded it behind a rock. His mother later realized it was missing and asked what had happened.

"I told her and she slapped me," Adnan said, still remembering the sting on his cheek. He was seldom punished. " 'That sack is how we'll survive,' she said and she walked back to get it."

Across the river in Jordan there were many fig trees along the bank. Beneath their branches in the shade, Adnan's mother started a fire and, with the flour, made bread.

"We were all so hungry," he said. "It was then that I realized how important carrying that sack was."

The next day, Jordanian trucks carried the refugees to Nablus. Many families lived in tents or in the classrooms of a school.

Three days later Abu Adnan found his family.

Although Abu was extremely fortunate to still have his truck, some supplies, and even a little money, he knew life would now be more treacherous than it had been in the carefree days on the mountain.

Abu chose to take his family to Syria because it was close to Ijzim; he was still certain that someday they'd return home. He bought a house in the countryside of Kiswe, about eight miles south of Damascus.

In the old city Adnan saw buildings and cars—many cars—for the very first time. In the past he had been familiar only with his father's truck and the village bus. "I thought this was like an adventure," Adnan said. "I could not understand my parents' sorrow."

But slowly Adnan began to notice that the family did not have what they used to. Now he had to cry and whine for things he'd always been given without asking. Even a small request for ice cream would often be refused.

His father opened a supermarket. Their life was better than that of a lot of Palestinians who had been displaced from their homes, but it was far from tranquil.

"All Arab countries opened their doors to the Palestinians," Adnan said. "But they did not treat us equally."

Among children playing, it was common for Syrians to tell the Palestinians, "You people sold your country to the Jews. You are weak."

"They were only repeating what they heard their parents say," Adnan said. "The Syrians looked at the Palestinians as though we were a disease."

Used as pawns in the established Arab regimes' conflict with Israel, the Palestinians became victims. By the time the fighting stopped in January 1949 and armistices were signed between Israel and the neighboring Arab states, 750,000 to 1 million Palestinians had fled their homes. Many had left after being urged to do so by Arab leaders; others had been forced to leave by the Jewish forces. Given the bitterly contested history of the Arab-Israeli conflict, it may never be known how many left on their volition and how many were driven out. Still, at the end of the 1949 fighting, not all Palestinians had been displaced; about 160,000 remained or were able to return to their homes in what was now Israeli territory.

For the majority of the Palestinians, the 1948 war became known in Arabic as the "Catastrophe." Of the Arabs displaced, most—more than half a million—became refugees in Jordan, primarily on the West Bank of the Jordan River. About 140,000 ended up as refugees in the Egypt-occupied Gaza Strip. The rest went to Lebanon and Syria, where most of them lived beset by squalor and deprived of the most basic human needs. For the Arab world, keeping the Palestinians in such putrid conditions kept the Arab-Israeli conflict alive. It became a festering sore that could be used to great advantage as the ruling elites directed the population's rage at their Jewish neighbor rather than let it focus on domestic problems. Palestinians were also the victims of racism among the other Arab populations; most were not allowed to integrate into Arab society. Nevertheless, some Palestinian families were able to escape the refugee trap and assimilate to some degree into their adopted countries. In time, Palestinians would become the most highly educated, per capita, of the Arab peoples.

In 1954, Adnan went to Damascus's Alliance High School, which was specifically designed for Palestinians. He was happy—too naïve to really know the difference between Syria and Palestine, but he recalls his mother and father often speaking about "our land" and "our money."

A local joke circulated among Palestinians about a fortune-teller who had said it would be seven days, seven weeks, or seven months before the Palestinians could return to their land.

"After seven *years* had passed, we asked, 'Maybe she meant seven *hundred* years?' " Adnan said.

When Adnan graduated from high school his parents

gave him a gift of a red-and-black motor scooter. He liked it but almost immediately wanted something bigger and faster. He rented a motorcycle and was promptly arrested for being under the driving age. He spent the night in jail.

Sometime between high school and joining the army a couple of years later, Adnan, who was mostly loafing around, met Adib Hobi, who owned a dry cleaner's in his neighborhood.

Hobi spoke of democracy and the difference between communism and freedom. Adnan had never thought about such concepts before nor had he witnessed such a passion for ideas.

Hobi didn't like dictators at a time when everyone in Syria was infatuated with Egyptian leader Gamal Abdel Nasser. Nasser had cultivated a widespread following throughout the Arab world for his willingness to stand up to the West. Hobi said Nasser was a communist and he, Hobi, wanted Syria to be democratic. Adnan was intrigued.

"Hobi went to jail many times for his thinking," Adnan said. "He opened my eyes to the world."

His parents complained that he was too young to be hanging around with Hobi, who was six or seven years older than he was, but Adnan didn't care.

Part of the knowledge Hobi shared with Adnan was about America. He watched American movies endlessly and read about democracy.

"The first American movie I saw was *Shazam,*" Adnan said.

But best of all, Adnan liked *Hollywood or Bust,* starring Jerry Lewis and Dean Martin. "I remember that car—a 1956 red Plymouth convertible," Adnan said. "And the scenery: warm, sunny, palm trees, it looked like heaven—

it looked like freedom. In my country, if you tell the police to get lost you get killed. But Lewis and Martin did anything they wanted."

Hobi painted a picture of America, democracy, and freedom in Adnan's head, but neither spoke about actually ever going there. It was too far away.

By the time Adnan was twenty, his parents had had enough of his carousing and espousing of Hobi's philosophy. Besides, his hand in marriage had been promised to his second cousin Selma, and she was quickly coming of age.

But Adnan had different plans. When he told his mother he didn't want to be married yet, she insisted that the oldest son had to be the first to have children.

He said he wanted to marry a woman like the neighborhood doctor's wife, who was German and had blond hair and blue eyes. His mother laughed and dismissed his reluctance as immaturity.

Fighting harder, he said that once he got married he'd be stuck and couldn't do the things he'd always wanted to. Still his parents would not listen to his arguments. Finally, he told them that he was scared he would do something bad, like commit adultery. His wife would also be a relative; he worried about the wrath of his uncles and feared a family schism.

His parents finally agreed that Adnan wasn't ready for marriage. They diplomatically dealt with their broken promise, which in itself was a serious insult, and Selma was married to Adnan's younger brother.

Adnan resumed listening to Hobi and bumming around with friends. He'd escaped marriage, he didn't work, and for lapses of time he never saw the sun.

"I was up all night, every night with my friends," he

said. "My father didn't like my behavior but he never said anything. He didn't have to. His eyes said it all."

Adnan threw his family name around. It had always kept him out of trouble in Ijzim and now it also worked well in Kiswe because his father was such a well-respected businessman. His friends were all handsome, debonair, and from good families, too. They took advantage of their parents' hard work, earning money through intimidation at the area bars they frequented.

"Establishments would give us a percentage so we wouldn't cause problems," Adnan said.

At Café Riyadh in Damascus one night in 1963, they demanded $300 for a month of no trouble. The management refused. "So later we went in and staged a fight with each other," Adnan said. "We broke chairs and windows and smashed televisions. Everybody respected us and were scared of us at the same time."

Once again his parents urged him to get married, this time to another cousin. "Leave me alone," he told them. "I'll get married when I decide to."

It was a clear sign of rejection when Adnan initially refused to get married. Turning down a second chance was too much for other family members not to take notice. Something was wrong with him, some said. One uncle suggested that Adnan was gay.

"At that point my mother got mad," he said. "She told people that she had heard about me being with several different girls. She said she cleaned my underwear and knew me well enough to know I wasn't gay."

The second cousin was married to another of Adnan's younger brothers.

Eventually the nightclub scene became tiresome. It was no longer a challenge, nor was it profitable enough.

Adnan wanted more money and more power.

He joined the Palestine Liberation Organization in 1965, a year after its founding. At the same time, the PLO established the Palestine Liberation Army, which was to be composed of young Palestinians who would be trained as a military force to attack Israel and Israeli targets. The Arab regimes, led by Egypt and Syria, would take the lead in creating military camps, where the young draftees would be trained in guerrilla subversion and terrorist acts. By law everyone was required to enroll in the service for two years, but Adnan figured that by signing up for five he could go to the academy and not just end up a lowly sergeant.

He spent nine months at the officer academy. It was tough, but Adnan thrived on each obstacle set before him. Part of the training included a forty-five-day survival camp.

"They killed dogs and would leave them in the sun to rot," he said. "We were expected to overcome our senses and pick them up with our teeth." They were placed in sewers for training exercises. Under the Palestine Liberation Army regulations, as recalled by Adnan, such was the latitude given to camp commanders that it was permissible if half of the students-in-training died.

In all of the tests, Adnan came out at the top of his class. When future Syrian President Hafez al-Assad, then an air-force lieutenant, visited the academy in 1966, Adnan was one of five students chosen to demonstrate what they had learned.

He made a name for himself as a captain in the Palestine Liberation Army at a Syrian army base in the area known as the "triangle"—where the borders of Israel, Jordan, and Syria all converge. He took all the dregs of the service—mostly enlisted men who did drugs, drank too much, or wanted to escape—and made them military police.

"But there was one thing I was constantly aware of," he said. "As part of the Palestinian army we were under Syrian government control and we were not free to say or think what we wanted."

For three years Adnan served faithfully, believing that his army was good and strong and that someday he would go back to his country.

But when Israel preemptively attacked Syria in the June 1967 Six-Day War, he became disillusioned. "We saw the Israeli planes—they played like birds above our heads," he said. "They were the only ones in the sky. It was like an air show."

The Six-Day War proved to be the most decisive victory that Israeli forces ever achieved over their Arab enemies. In May, Egyptian President Nasser had imposed a blockade on Israel's only outlet to the Red Sea, the port of Aqaba. He ordered the U.N. peacekeeping forces withdrawn from the Sinai and mobilized tens of thousands of Egyptian troops on the Israeli border. Following suit, Syria amassed its forces on the strategic Golan Heights border overlooking Israel's north—a vantage point from which the Syrians had shelled Israeli farmers for years. On June 5, the Israelis struck first, knocking out the Egyptian air force on the ground in a matter of hours. The entire Sinai Peninsula was captured, as were the Golan Heights and the West Bank of Jordan. It was a devastating defeat for the Arab world.

Adnan began to sense that he was being lied to. Arab radio reported that Arabs everywhere were heroically fighting and winning the battle against the Jews but Adnan knew that he and his troops had yet to fire a gun.

"In reality, the war that the Arabs said lasted six days was over in six hours," Adnan said. "The Israelis defeated Egypt, Syria, and Jordan. She took us all on before we even got our planes off the ground."

Another detail that puzzled Adnan, who had been steeped in propaganda that Israel was trying to take over the entire Arab world, was that even when the Arabs' defense was all but invisible, Israel was not greedy about what it was fighting for. In fact, it was very specific.

"She only took the Golan, the Sinai, and the West Bank," Adnan said. "She could have easily taken Damascus if she wanted."

This forced Adnan to look at his government from an entirely different perspective. "I finally understood," Adnan said. "All along the Arab governments make believe that we have power, that we are strong, and that we are against Israel, but it is not really Israel that these governments are fighting. They are against their own people gaining power. They are afraid of democracy and they have to maintain control."

His unhappiness grew to contempt.

"I had gone into the army because it was power," he said. "Power for the people, not the enemy. But we were a paper army—and I began hating it and myself."

Constantly rebelling against authority and seeking the preferential treatment that he had always received as a child, Adnan angered his superiors.

Major Hussein Adra banned him from driving his Fiat on the army base. Adnan complained to his grandmother that the major was jealous because he had to drive a dirty Jeep. His grandmother went above the major's head and, with a note from General Assad Dabor, got her grandson special permission to drive his car on the base. Another time, he missed ten days of duty but avoided punishment with a letter from a colonel—a letter that entitled him to even more time off. Such antics did not endear him to his superiors.

He tried to get discharged but couldn't. When he finally finished his five-year commitment, the army wanted to keep him longer.

Not surprisingly, he got a doctor friend to write a note that he was suffering from asthma, and Adnan was released from duty in December 1969.

He was offered a position in Lebanon, and from 1970 to 1971 he worked there for the Fedayeen, the Palestinian terrorists who infiltrated Israel to attack and murder Israeli civilians. But he didn't have much respect for the position or his responsibilities. Part of his lasting rebellion from the army was a hardened cynicism toward his government. He recruited girlfriends and put them on government salaries. He flippantly handed out I.D.'s that would allow passage across the border. One such I.D. was given to a man who later killed someone inside Beirut. When he was arrested he gave the police the pass with Adnan's signature on it.

Adnan was promptly fired, and he returned to Damascus.

"I didn't care because now I had my passport, my freedom," he said. Palestinians were generally denied passports by the Arab countries in which they resided.

Convincing his mother that he could make a lot of money importing cars from Germany, Adnan got her to invest $10,000, and he started a business. He made four or five trips to Germany and, in between, spent his time traveling, visiting friends, and publicly criticizing the military government of Syria.

One day he was stopped in a restaurant by Syrian President Assad's brother, Colonel Rifaat al-Assad, who was in charge of Syria's special military forces. He said, "Listen, if you don't shut up I'll cut your tongue out."

"What did I do?" Adnan said, but he knew what he'd done.

He was willing to tell anyone who cared to listen, and even those who would rather not, about why he was no longer in the service. He angrily accused the army of being filled with communists and he spoke openly against the Syrian president and his brother.

Friends and family told him to leave the country before something happened to him. An acquaintance offered him a lot of money to move to Abu Dhabi, the capital of the United Arab Emirates, where he had a construction business and could use Adnan's help.

Besides bad-mouthing the army and the president's brother, Adnan had been making many trips back and forth to Iraq—considered the enemy of Syria—visiting officer friends who had abandoned their duty and escaped. (Even today, when the army has forgotten about his insolence, the government suspects him of having been a spy because of the time he spent consorting with Iraqis in Baghdad.)

The Syrian intelligence agency was investigating him. Adnan knew he could face imprisonment at best and a slow, painful death at worst. So in 1975 he left Syria for good.

2

Abu Dahab (Father of Gold)

Adnan was happy with the money and new life his friend
generously arranged for him in Abu Dhabi. But soon he
thought he could do better than driving a Datsun.

Figuring there was enough money for everyone to be a
millionaire during the petrodollar boom in the Persian
Gulf, he began to scheme. His friend spoke ceaselessly of
a Prince Ghasem Khalifa, someone who supposedly had
many businesses and hired lots of people. In fact, Adnan's
friend had a few construction contracts with him that had
proved to be lucrative. This prince, he said, was extremely
accessible, spent money extravagantly, and liked to party
and have fun with girls. And he drove a car the likes of
which Adnan had never seen before. Everything that was
normally made of nickel, including the hub of the steering
wheel and the exhaust pipes, was gold. "I thought, 'This
is a man I would like to meet myself,' " Adnan said.

So he decided he'd paint a picture for the prince. It
depicted two gazelles drinking from a pond at sunset. In
the background, a hunter tried to shoot while another
prevented him. The message was one of Arab honor: You

don't do anything behind an animal's or a person's back. You meet your challenge face-to-face.

He brought the painting to the prince's servant—a man from Yemen—whose sole responsibility was taking care of a female camel. The camel was prized for her milk because it was thought to provide endurance during sex. The servant promised to deliver the painting to Kalifa. Two days later the servant found Adnan and gave him an envelope containing $2,500.

"I refused it," Adnan said. "I told him that the painting was a gift and I did not expect money." The next day the servant returned. The prince had requested to see him. When they met, the prince said, "You are looking for something—I can see it in your eyes. What do you want?"

Adnan replied, "This is a big city and I am capable of doing many things. I want a job that will pay me a lot of money."

The prince agreed to employee him, asking him to rent a big apartment in Dubai. He said he'd pay for everything but it had to be in Adnan's name. Adnan found a place on Circle Gamal Abdel Nasser. "I remember the carpet was green," Adnan said. "He wanted everything green— even the refrigerator. I almost died but instead I said it was a beautiful color. He told me we'd have fun and do business together."

Adnan started off as the prince's chauffeur, but soon the prince asked Adnan to manage the city's black-market liquor concession, which he controlled. For the most part, the purchase and consumption of liquor was prohibited in the Islamic world. Alcohol was permitted only in the major hotels in Abu Dhabi. When Adnan asked how he could do such a job without going to jail, the prince assured him that nothing would happen because the chief of police was his partner. He explained the arrangement: He was responsible for bringing the whiskey in by ship, the chief then brought it to the storage area, and Adnan would organize its distribution. To prove there was nothing to fear, the prince introduced Adnan to Chief Alhadidi and gave him a tour of the storage area, which was located just outside of the city.

After a few months of this work—"fifty cases here and there within the city"—the prince told Adnan he had done a good job and was ready for a promotion. Now he would be in charge of the distribution of all the alcohol going into Saudi Arabia. It was a big operation. Trucks would carry four hundred to five hundred cases at a time over the border. Adnan no longer drove a Datsun. A flashy Camaro had always been more his style; now he could easily afford it.

"I had wads of hundred-dollar bills in my pocket and people said, 'My God, he just got here,'" Adnan remembers. "Soon I earned the nickname of Abu Dahab—Father of Gold."

His apartment on Circle Gamal Abdel Nasser was the home of a constant party. They'd drink potent licorice-tasting arak and smoke piles of hashish, and women would come in via private planes from all over the world. The prince would call a madame with a list of what nationality girls he wanted, including specifications of eye color, hair color, and height. "He would pay a lot of money for them," Adnan said. "Sometimes they were very young, like thirteen years old, virgins that their fathers had sold to the prince for thousands of dollars." Such debauchery was referred to as "red nights," and Adnan was sworn never to mention anything about them for fear that the prince's wife would catch on.

On one such red night the prince gave Adnan a young Egyptian girl. Her name was Fatima and she was fourteen. Tall, with coffee skin, she had long black straight hair and almond-shaped, honey-colored eyes. But when Adnan began to kiss her she cried. She said that she had been married to a man who lied to her family that he was a successful businessman. His business was primarily selling her. "I thought she was a whore," Adnan said. "This took me by surprise and I told her not to worry, that we'd sleep in the same bed as though we were brother and sister." The next day he gave her the address of the Egyptian consulate. He told her to go there and never go back to her husband again.

Adnan started traveling and splashing his money throughout the Middle East. He would drive the thousand miles from Abu Dhabi to Baghdad—passing through three countries—just to hang out at the Moulin Rouge cabaret. He met a lot of people on the fast track and in 1975 started dating a showgirl. The life-style she described was alluring. She was from Spain and said there were a lot of investments to be made. She invited him to come with her. "There was money everywhere," Adnan said. "But I needed more."

He told the prince he wanted to leave the United Arab Emirates. The prince advised him not to go, but Adnan wouldn't listen. He transferred all of his money into thirty-six kilos of gold: twenty-four cubes and twelve kilos in handmade Indian jewelry with elaborate filigree work and gems. After packing his car with all of his clothes and a briefcase filled with four different currencies, and with the gold stashed in between the front seats, he started the long drive.

Unbeknownst to him, on the day he began his journey a terrorist from Syria blew up a mosque in Iraq. Adnan was traveling with a Syrian passport, and when he got to the border of Iraq he was met with great suspicion—especially since his passport showed that he traveled so frequently between countries and he was driving an expensive car when most people had only Soviet and Eastern bloc imports that perpetually broke down.

"Bad, stupid luck," he said. "They checked every piece of the car and when they found the gold I thought, 'I am going to jail for the rest of my life.'" The security people asked him why he hadn't claimed the gold on the customs form. He told them the truth, which in this case was so farfetched it would have been better to lie. He explained that he was going to Baghdad to run away with a cabaret girl to Spain, where he would start his life over.

He was placed under arrest and the security chief told him he needed a lawyer. Adnan gave the chief $100 to find him one. After three nights in jail in Basra, the port city on the Iraq-Iran border, Adnan was bailed out by the lawyer. During his trial the judge decided that he would have to pay a $10,000 fine for trying to smuggle gold across the border, and his prized possession, the car, was confiscated.

Outside of the courtroom, the reality of losing most of his money and belongings began to sink in. He decided to go to his sister's in Baghdad for help. For the first time in his life he traveled by bus, with chickens, goats, and other animals riding atop. The three-hundred-mile trip took twenty-four hours. He arrived around midnight and stopped by the cabaret to explain to his lover that he could no longer accompany her to Spain. "I just can't make it in another country with no money to start me off," he told her. She pleaded with him to come anyway, but he said good-bye. At his sister's he picked up some money to return to Basra, where he had to pay his fine and retrieve his passport, which had been held as collateral. He decided that he could not return to Abu Dhabi. The prince and others had told him not to leave and he had not heeded anyone's advice. "I had lost everything. I didn't want anyone to see me this way. In Basra, nobody knew me," he said. "I charged myself one year in my own kind of jail: no drinking, no women, just hard work." He checked into a $3-a-night hotel with a room the size of a bathroom.

He searched for a job, never ate out in restaurants, never socialized. He met some Egyptians who said they could get him a job as a truck driver. The next day he showed up for work at Yamazaki, a Japanese multinational construction firm. He was paid $400 a week. "I used to give that amount as a tip at the cabaret," he said. "But I didn't complain." His expensive dress set him apart from the other workers, and the management immediately took notice.

The owner of the business, a man named Nichochi, told him, "Something has happened to you. Something is not right. The way you clean your hands, the way the dirt on your shoes bothers you." Adnan took the opportunity to ask Nichochi for overtime work. His wish was granted. He would pick up all the drivers, bring them to work, and at the end of the day he would drop them all off. He never was late. Soon he was asked to be a chauffeur for the manager, Mr. Adaka. They got along well and Adnan would accompany him on all business trips. But when

Adaka wanted to go to Baghdad to see the cabaret, Adnan refused. "I told him that everyone in the cabaret knew me when I was rich and now I am a driver," Adnan said. "So he made a deal with me. He gave me the money to pay for everything and we'd pretend that his car was mine." When the manager saw the reception Adnan received at the cabaret he was impressed and gave him more responsibilities. After a year in Basra, Adnan had saved $3,000. He moved out of the hotel and into an apartment. He told his friends at Yamazaki that he had to quit to plan his future. He bought a taxi for his own transportation as well as to bring in extra money. He started a small construction business and painted schools. Soon he had government contracts and fifty employees. "I sold the taxi and had a Chevrolet Nova, a Dodge Monaco, and finally a Mercedes," he said. "I started to feel as though I had wings again."

But bad luck followed him. When the war between Iran and Iraq started in 1980, all of his construction contracts were halted and business flagged. Then Mr. Adaka appeared on his doorstep, come to ask if Adnan would do some work for the Japanese firm in Baghdad. He agreed. After a quick trip to Japan he moved to Baghdad. Soon he was making more money than he had while working for the prince in Dubai.

One of his most interesting projects was a 1981 government contract to build a secret palace and bunker for President Saddam Hussein in Lake Habbaniya, a resort area thirty miles west of Baghdad frequented by Iraqi officers. The area had been initially developed by the British during World War II. As site manager, Adnan oversaw the construction of a lavish vacation home for Hussein and a three-story fortified underground bunker beneath the house. Thick stainless-steel doors sealed off each room in the bunker; generators were built to bring in air from the outside, making possible extensive underground stays for Hussein and his family. A secret exit to an airfield was also built.

Adnan now lived in a three-bedroom villa and owned several cars, keeping thousands of dollars under the front seats. Very important and wealthy people were now coming to him, among them Hussein's son, who bought Adnan's Datsun 280Z.

"People thought I was Superman," he said. "I had more than two million dollars in the bank, five cars, a house, and a beautiful young girlfriend. Everything would have been fine, but I met up with stupid people."

Sitting in the lobby of the Al Salaam hotel in Baghdad, Adnan ran into a friend he hadn't seen in three years, since they'd both been truck drivers at Yamazaki. His name was Abdul Razzak el-Nashashibi and he was Palestinian too. They had lived in the same hotel and both had been broke, but, like Adnan, Nashashibi was from a wealthy and well-known family. Their stories were much alike. "I was so poor and he was so poor," Adnan said. "And we had similar habits. He was crazy about women and money."

After their initial reunion they saw each other every night for two weeks. Nashashibi, about forty-five and balding, explained that he was based in Thailand doing some sort of import work. It was a great job that paid him well. Adnan wanted to share his wealth and treated his old friend to fabulous restaurants and the cabaret. Nashashibi was amazed by his largesse.

He left for a couple of weeks to touch base in Thailand but when he returned he brought Adnan many beautiful gifts: snakeskin shoes, leather luggage, and perfume for

Adnan's girlfriend, Ronac. Adnan offered to pay for the items but Nashashibi refused.

After about an hour he asked if Adnan could do a favor for him. Adnan said, "Sure, whatever you want." Nashashibi needed a ride to a friend's. "This is not a favor. Ask me for a bigger one next time," Adnan told him. On the way, Nashashibi spoke very highly of this man. They drove along the winding streets south of Baghdad to an area called Al-Mansour. The neighborhood was home to wealthy Iraqis, elite army officers, and foreign consulates.

"Do I know this friend?" Adnan asked. Nashashibi said no, that he was an old Palestinian friend whom he'd grown up with in Jerusalem. "He told me that he was a captain," Adnan said. "I got excited and said, 'I was a captain in the Palestinian army and I know almost all of the officers. Who is it?" But Nashashibi just smiled and said, "I don't think you know him. He is a captain in the Fedayeen, not the army. His name is Mohammed Rashid."

3

Becoming a "Hero"

In an instant, Adnan knew exactly what Mohammed Rashid was a captain of: terrorism. In Arab countries, terrorism is publicly acceptable and terrorists are given military titles, although they are not officially in the legitimate army. "Terrorism is a business in Iraq," Adnan said. "It's so commonplace to have a job as a terrorist that I wasn't shocked when Abdul told me that's what his friend did. I didn't think to judge him. But at the same time I had no idea of the extent of his reputation nor the destruction he caused."

The front door of Mohammed Rashid's house was opened by a handsome, thin man in his early thirties with dark hair, a mustache, and penetrating eyes. "Adnan, this is Captain Mohammed Rashid," Nashashibi said.

Rashid was visibly disturbed. "I've told you a thousand times never to use that name! Security reasons," he said, glaring at Nashashibi, who quickly explained that Adnan was a close friend and a Palestinian.

Rashid then apologized. "I'm being cautious because I'm wanted by the Mossad [the Israeli intelligence agency]," he explained. Adnan didn't think twice about it. Freedom fighters were always at risk.

"Terrorists are heroes in Iraq," Adnan says. "They go to cabaret in their camouflage clothes. Rashid seemed like a nice guy and he was from my country. His profession was none of my business."

Mohammed's wife, Fatima, was there, along with their two-year-old son, Zuhair. Fatima was nearly six feet tall and skinny. She had a long, thin nose, freckles, and blond straight hair that reached midway down her back. She spoke Arabic but with a strong European accent. Adnan wasn't surprised to see her instead of a traditional Arab bride. Many terrorists associate themselves with European women because they look less suspicious.

With the initial uneasiness resolved, both Rashid and Fatima were very cordial. Their living room was lined with built-in bookshelves that contained decorative objects from all over the world. Nashashibi was clearly comfortable, even helping himself to what was in their refrigerator. The four talked for a couple of hours. When Nashashibi said it was time to go, Fatima suggested that Adnan come over again with his girlfriend. Adnan agreed.

Later Nashashibi explained that he too worked for the Fedayeen—and not in the import business, as he had originally said. He was in charge of finding safe houses—different stations in Germany, Australia, Thailand, and England where terrorists could rest in between missions rather than jeopardize their security in hotels. He praised Rashid for his bravery, saying that he had been the mastermind of a lot of Fedayeen operations. That was why he had earned the rank of captain even though he had never gone to the military academy. There were too many Fedayeen groups for Adnan to keep track. All that mattered to him was that Rashid and his wife would be fun to socialize with.

Adnan and Ronac were guests at Mohammed Rashid's house several times. They all got along very well. They picnicked in a park on the banks of the Diyala River. They went out to eat. It was during one of these visits that Ronac asked Fatima how she got so many foreign magazines that were unavailable in Iraq. Fatima bragged that she traveled often. Later she showed Ronac and Adnan three passports: one Austrian, another Lebanese, and the third Iraqi.

She was proud of them. (The CIA would later find out that Fatima's real name was Christine Pinter and she had been born in Austria.) Another time she brought Ronac upstairs and showed her the pistol, a Browning 9mm with a fourteen-round clip, that she kept under her pillow.

Ronac was shocked. Having a gun was a serious offense in Iraq. Adnan was curious to know how Fatima felt about her husband's profession, so he asked Rashid. "She loves me and she loves the job," he said. "She usually comes with me." He mentioned that she even collected news clippings of their successful missions.

Ronac and Adnan discussed their new friends' eccentricities but they didn't feel that was enough of a reason to stop seeing them.

At a gathering at Rashid's on the afternoon of June 6, 1982, Adnan was introduced to Rashid's boss. A short, stout Palestinian in his fifties with a mustache and dressed in plain military-style khakis, this man's name was Abu Ibrahim.

"He looked cold-blooded," Adnan remembers. His deep voice was the sort that commanded respect; clearly he was used to being listened to and obeyed. Ibrahim was there with his wife and son. Adnan could tell that he was deeply religious, as he didn't smoke or drink.

Everyone was watching television when one news item triggered heated political discussion. Israeli forces had just launched a massive operation to rid Lebanon of the armed Palestinian terrorist presence, which for years had shelled Israeli towns and settlements in the north with Katyusha rockets and had directed terrorist attacks across the border. The terrorists had killed scores of Israeli civilians and had made the entire north of Israel an unstable and dangerous place.

For the past year, however, there had been a de facto truce with the PLO and the Palestinians had held their fire. Still, the prospect of 10,000 armed members of the Palestine Liberation Organization, equipped with enough small arms, tanks, rockets, rocket-propelled grenades, artillery, and explosives for more than a 500,000-man army, did not make Israel feel at ease. When the Israeli ambassador to Great Britain, Shlomo Argov, was shot in the head in early June 1982 by Palestinian terrorists in London, the Israelis had a pretext for eliminating the Palestinian threat.

More than 100,000 Israeli troops had crossed the Lebanese border, fighting their way up the coast to Beirut. Israeli bombers attacked PLO positions in Sidon, Tyre, and Beirut. In fact, because the PLO had placed its artillery and antiaircraft guns in the middle of Lebanese civilian centers and Palestinian refugee camps, Israeli bombers had attacked targets in downtown Beirut as well as the camps. Television cameras recorded the merciless Israeli pounding, then broadcast it around the world.

Abu Ibrahim got very excited now when he saw scenes of the Israeli onslaught. He spoke of reclaiming Palestine, promising to pay the Israelis back for their invasion with a trail of bloody terrorist acts.

"How can we stay here when our brothers are dying in Lebanon?" he asked. "It's not fair that we are living the good life."

Adnan agreed, saying that it was pathetic that the overwhelmingly superior Israeli army had attacked the far weaker Fedayeen groups in Lebanon. To Adnan, the talk reflected social camaraderie among Palestinians, not premeditated political theory. Later Ibrahim turned to Adnan and asked if he'd help the cause.

"I said yes, but I wasn't taking it seriously," Adnan recalled. "I was being conversational and didn't really think I'd ever see the man again."

The encounter left a lasting impression on Adnan. He was offended by Ibrahim's abrasive demeanor and piety yet he recognized that the man had some strange sort of magnetism.

Adnan and Ronac continued to see Rashid and Fatima. They were at an ice cream parlor together a few days later when Rashid pulled Adnan aside and mentioned that Ibrahim's office was very close by. Would he like to stop in? Adnan said sure.

They drove to a different area of the Al-Mansour neighborhood and pulled up outside what looked like someone's home. Adnan knew it wasn't Ibrahim's because Rashid had once mentioned that Ibrahim lived in northern Baghdad, where senior and elite government officials resided. Besides, an unfamiliar family name, ABDULAZIZ, was on an entrance plaque. When they got inside, Adnan could see that this was not a home at all. There was barely any furniture; there were no personal belongings. It was obviously a safe house, like the ones Nashashibi had told him about. This was Ibrahim's headquarters.

In what Adnan perceived as an uncharacteristically gentle voice, Ibrahim told Adnan that it was time for him to do something for his people and Palestine.

Adnan said, "Sure—how much money would you like? I'll write a check."

Ibrahim told him that money was not what the "cause" needed. "We have plenty of money," he said. "We need fighters. We must do something on our own, since the Arab countries are unwilling to do anything to help our Palestinian brothers."

He explained that Adnan was perfect because he was Palestinian and also older than most of the other terrorists. He looked respectable and wealthy. He spoke a little English, traveled a lot, had never been to Europe, and his army experience meant that he would be able to handle pressure situations. "We don't have the time to train someone else," he said, his voice growing sterner now. "We need to shake the world with many missions at the same time and I want you to help." The request sounded more like a demand.

Adnan said something noncommittal and somebody changed the subject. Rashid later told Adnan that Ibrahim was a powerful man. "He could hold me and all the rest of us in one hand," he said.

The next day Ibrahim called Adnan and asked again for his participation. Adnan told him that he didn't believe in launching attacks against civilians. He thought it was cowardice and said that he thought armies should fight face-to-face with other legitimate armies.

The somewhat pleasant façade Ibrahim had been maintaining since their first meeting quickly evaporated. "It's Palestinians like yourself," he said, "who only care about making money, who are not willing to sacrifice for their country." Ibrahim again pressed Adnan to go on a mission. Uncomfortable, Adnan refused. They hung up, Adnan vowing he wouldn't ever go back to see Ibrahim again.

Frightened and angry, Adnan drove to the hotel where Nashashibi was staying. "Why did you do this to me?" he demanded furiously.

Nashashibi said he thought he was doing him a favor. Ibrahim, he said, would make him rich and powerful. Adnan said he was already rich and didn't want to be involved. Nashashibi tried to calm him down, telling Adnan that he would be famous.

"To Abdul this was just a job," Adnan said. "In fact, as long as I knew him he had never had a problem with Jews. He only spoke of women and money. This was not a Palestinian commitment, it was an economic one. To me the proposition meant much more."

Nashashibi told Adnan that the decision about doing business with Ibrahim was up to him. He said that Rashid and Ibrahim had investigated Adnan and found that he could be trusted.

It was around this time that Nashashibi introduced Adnan to his cousin Marwar, visiting from Israel, where he said he was a spy. Adnan finally admitted to himself that he had inadvertently gotten involved with the wrong group of people. Now, everywhere he turned he was surrounded by so-called freedom fighters.

Adnan tried to avoid further contact with Ibrahim. He didn't return his messages. Ronac screened calls at his office and made sure never to let anyone know where he was. But four days later an emergency call came through from Adnan's foreman.

Adnan's employees had been working for three months on a multimillion-dollar government contract, building warehouses at El Rashid—a classified military base in Baghdad. The foreman said now that the sixty workers had suddenly been banned from entering the base, even though they had three more months' worth of work to go.

Adnan immediately drove to the base to speak to the security officer. "What the hell is going on?" Adnan asked him. "You'll have to speak with Abu Ibrahim," was all he was told. "But I have a contract with the government!" Adnan protested. His pleas fell on deaf ears. "There's nothing I can do—I have my orders. Go speak with Abu Ibrahim to settle this," the officer responded.

"I suddenly realized," Adnan says, "that if Ibrahim could stop me from entering a military base, his power was far stronger than mine. He could break me. Anyone who has power within a dictatorship government can do a lot—and it was clear Ibrahim had high membership." Even if he fled Iraq, leaving his business behind, Ibrahim could track him down.

"This is not a man that you reason with," Adnan thought to himself. "You just do as he says."

Adnan was trapped. The business he had worked so hard to build—from absolutely nothing—was at stake. If Ibrahim could prevent him from working on a government contract, there was no way Adnan would be able to maintain any other contracts. Beyond the repercussions to his business, Adnan sensed there was a larger danger; he feared for his life. It became increasingly obvious that he would have to speak with Ibrahim again.

Ibrahim's true name was Hussein Mohammed al-Umari and he was born in Haifa, Palestine, around 1936. During the 1948 Arab-Israeli war, his family fled north to Lebanon and then to Syria. A university graduate, Abu Ibrahim became a follower of George Habash, a radical Palestinian doctor who championed a secular Marxist Palestinian movement that fiercely opposed the very existence of the state of Israel.

Habash's Damascus-based group, the Popular Front for the Liberation of Palestine, was a particularly violent organization that masterminded some of the most notorious terrorist acts in the past twenty-five years. The most infamous was a quadruple airplane hijacking in 1970. Three American planes were blown up in a massive explosion at a former British air base in Jordan. The fourth plane was commandeered and flown to Cairo.

Habash himself never got involved in the operational planning of terror attacks. That was left up to his right-hand man, Waddi Haddad, who had engineered the 1970 hijacking extravaganza. In the mid-1970s, Haddad formed his own terrorist group, known as the Popular Front for the Liberation of Palestine—Special Operations Group, and set up his headquarters in Iraq. Haddad took with him several of Habash's followers, including Abu Ibrahim, who became one of Haddad's chief deputies, responsible for the detailed planning of terrorist operations. Ibrahim went to East Germany and the Soviet Union, where he was trained in handling explosives and demolitions, bomb making, and other aspects of terrorist warfare.

In July 1976, Haddad's group—largely due to the energies of Abu Ibrahim—captured the world's attention when they hijacked an Air France Airbus and flew it to Entebbe Airport in Uganda. Haddad's international crew of terrorists separated the Jewish passengers from the others, prompting Israel to launch the most daring counter-terrorist rescue ever.

Though defeated, Haddad continued to launch attacks on Jews and Israelis in Europe. But in 1978, he died from an inoperable brain tumor. In the aftermath of his death, a U.S. Defense Department report would later note, his group splintered into three different organizations: the Popular Front for the Liberation of Palestine—Special Command; the Lebanese Armed Revolutionary Faction; and the May 15 Organization, named after the date on which the state of Israel was founded.

Abu Ibrahim became the leader of the May 15 Organization. In the next four years he developed a reputation among Western antiterrorist agencies as one of the most ruthless and obsessed terrorists in the world. Still, little was known about him.

Now Adnan was in his clutches.

As he sped to the safe house in Al-Mansour, Adnan's mind was racing in tandem with his car's engine. He wanted to extricate himself entirely from the terrorists but didn't know how it could be done delicately. The truth was inconsequential; objecting because he valued human life had been ineffective. Certainly, insulting them by condemning their philosophy was not a good tactic. Yet what was the perfect argument?

The peaceful neighborhoods with their tree-lined calm and order only made him more restless and aware of the chaos inside his head. His subconscious would barely acknowledge that he'd already been roped in by an evil genius and there was no escaping. Yet for the first time in his life, he felt desperately afraid, with no one to turn to. Adnan, the master of his own destiny, had lost control of his life.

When he arrived at the safe house, Ibrahim gave him a warm hello, as if nothing had happened. But Adnan didn't play along. He couldn't hide his fear and anger. Even though he was afraid of Ibrahim, Adnan let him have it. "What the hell are you doing to me?!"

Ibrahim's expression instantly turned from one of warmth to one of fury. Adnan persisted, asking why his workers had been banned from the military base. There was fire in Ibrahim's face now and Adnan knew he had pushed him to a flash point—but there was no retreating.

"All you care about is your money!" Ibrahim shot back. "But you are nothing! I can destroy you! You must help your people!" The words hung in the air. In Adnan's mind, he was hearing "I can destroy you!" over and over again.

Confronted with Ibrahim's wrath, Adnan knew rational arguments would be of no use. What could he say or do that would change Ibrahim's mind? He instantly decided that he would try the opposite approach.

"Perhaps you are right," he said slowly to Ibrahim. "It is my destiny—I must help out the cause."

Adnan knew that once that was said, he was going to have to prove it.

Adnan attempted to convince Ibrahim that he was now willing to do as he wished. But in the back of his mind, Adnan was sure he could later resolve the problem by proving himself incapable of carrying out Ibrahim's request.

His plan worked for the moment. Ibrahim calmed down. But never again would Ibrahim be as kind to Adnan as he had been before. This was a business deal that Adnan had been forced to accept and there were no negotiable terms.

The terrorist offered Adnan tea and began telling him about his specific mission. He would go to Switzerland to blow up the Noga Hilton in Geneva. The owner, he said, was Jewish and gave a lot of money to Israel.

"What about the other guests in the hotel?" Adnan asked.

"Our enemies are also Americans and the rich Arabs who dare to patronize this Zionist hotel," Ibrahim explained. His intelligence operatives had given him information to support his statements. They had canvassed the hotel only weeks before and returned with a detailed description of its layout and clientele and conversations overheard. They had pictures of members of the Saudi royal Family in traditional dress, photos of the front desk, and pamphlets from the hotel.

Then Ibrahim took a key from his pocket and led Adnan to a locked door. The room behind it made this safe house different from all others. It was an office of sorts, more like a workshop. Ibrahim went straight to a desk that had a few papers strewn on top. Above it was a gold-framed picture of a young handsome man. In a half moon below, in beautifully inscribed Arabic, it said, *In memory of Mohammed Zuhair, who died in the bombing of the Royal Hotel.*

On January 17, 1980, London's posh Mount Royal Hotel had been the site of Abu Ibrahim's first operation as head of the newly formed May 15 Organization. Mohammed Zuhair, a twenty-one-year-old Iraqi of Palestinian origin, had been dispatched by Ibrahim to bomb the hotel because it was known to have Jewish guests. Zuhair had traveled from Baghdad, via a European country, to London with the components of the bomb concealed in his suitcase, along with several kilos of plastic explosives. He had rented a room on the center of the fifth floor—a room carefully selected to ensure that the explosion would cause as much structural damage as possible. If things went as planned, the entire hotel would have come down like a house of cards—a strategy that Abu Ibrahim would try to replicate in future operations. But things did not go as planned; the bomb Zuhair had been preparing exploded prematurely. He was killed instantly. Several hotel guests were injured.

"I remember thinking," Adnan said, " 'I've heard of Fatah and other terrorist groups, but never May 15.' " He was well aware of the significance of the date, however; it was a black day in the minds and memories of many Palestinians.

Ibrahim noticed Adnan staring at the picture and told him that Rashid had named his son after this brave man. Adnan looked around the room. More than twenty pieces of luggage in different shapes, sizes, and subdued colors were lined up against the wall like soldiers at attention.

There was also a heavy-duty sewing machine and strips of fabric, a steel filing cabinet, and an iron safe with a device that looked like a battery charger on top. The odd combination of equipment confused him. "We use the house for operations, and the luggage for our missions," Ibrahim said nonchalantly.

He sat down, inviting Adnan to join him. The story he told over the next hour was horrifying to his unwilling "hero," who would soon be sent to kill under the mis-guided ambition of reclaiming Palestine. Ibrahim said that he had invented a bomb—one that was like no other. Adnan was familiar with explosives from his days in the army. He didn't dare interrupt, but he asked himself, "How different could this bomb be?"

Ibrahim continued in his low, powerful voice. He had discovered a way of concealing a bomb in the lining of a suitcase that would escape all detection by X ray, physical search, even scent dogs. It all sounded too weird to Adnan. Would Ibrahim seriously put the lives of his men on the line in the hopes that one of his bombs would somehow make it through airport security? The percentages seemed too low for such a high-risk endeavor.

There was no way Abu Ibrahim could have perceived Adnan's misgivings. He was too caught up in his own genius. He pointed to the sewing machine and said that it was used to put the suitcase back together again after replacing the cardboard frame with sheets of dark plastic that disguised the explosives. He pulled out a sheet to show Adnan, who couldn't believe he was actually looking at a bomb. The explosives were comprised of narrow strips as thin as amandeen—the pressed apricot and fig primarily eaten during the month of Ramadan. They had no odor and looked as innocuous as the cardboard frame they had replaced. Embedded in the strips was gold-plated nickel wire.

Even if the suitcase's lining was torn apart, Ibrahim said, the bomb would not be detected. The detonator was powered by AAA batteries. This was his secret, he told Adnan, and this was the reason his terrorists were the best. It was why the government trusted him. It was why he was so powerful. His eyes were intense.

Ibrahim's anger manifested itself in passion as he described his inventions of destruction. He said that their number one target and enemy was Israel. Their second was the United States, for helping the country that should not exist. He showed Adnan exactly how the bomb worked, lining up the strips of five hundred milligrams of plastic explosives end to end, then attaching them to a detonator that looked like no more than a battery charger for a razor. All together there were nearly seven pounds of explosives hidden in the suitcase. Abu Ibrahim told Adnan to use the razor blade to get the explosives out of the bag and to set them up, as he had demonstrated, underneath the mattress. He advised Adnan to glue the luggage back together after he took the strips of explosives out so the police would never suspect their method. "It's my invisible bomb," he said.

"My God," Adnan thought. "This is really serious." It was now dawning on him that he was stuck in the middle of a situation in which people would surely get killed.

His mouth was dry and his foot fell asleep. He tried to joke, telling Ibrahim that he didn't want to go to the airport carrying the light-beige bag with the detonator and the large piece of dark-tan luggage filled with explosives. "They're really ugly," he said. "They look cheap. How about if I take my own suitcase?"

Ibrahim laughed and said it had to be a particular type of luggage because that was the only kind that could conceal the explosives. Adnan knew that there was no escaping.

Ibrahim also told him the rules to avoid arousing suspicion. He was not to speak with other Arabs, not to read political magazines, and was never to look behind him. Those rules were repeated two or three times. "Most important," Ibrahim said, "don't rush. If I think there is a one percent chance for a mistake, we don't do the mission," he went on. "These missions have been planned for *months* before they are executed."

Over the next few weeks, Adnan saw Ibrahim more than twenty times as they finalized arrangements. He also saw Rashid, who bragged about blowing up the El Al airline office in Istanbul while the Mossad looked on, unaware. He said that he stuck a note on the back of an Israeli officer's jacket with a wisecrack written on it about the Mossad. Adnan didn't know if Rashid was making this up, but he did believe him when he said that the May 15 Organization had conducted successful bombings around the world. They had killed the "Zionist" enemy, Rashid said, who were such a big part of the conspiracy to kill all Arabs. Still, as much as Rashid was a true believer, he was also human—his and his wife's life-style showed that money and possessions were things to be desired in life.

Adnan confided in Rashid that he was worried about his business and did not want to go. Rashid told him that everything would be taken care of—he would personally ask Ibrahim to make sure to send Adnan to a nice place before he returned home. He also shared a secret: He too was leaving soon on a mission, several days before Adnan was to go. "You should do what he says," Rashid said. "He'll make sure nothing happens to you."

There were so many things to be done, so many errands to complete, in such a short amount of time. Most important, Adnan needed a new passport. Ibrahim mentioned that since Adnan was now his friend, Adnan's business would be certain to boom. All Ibrahim had to do, he said, was talk to the government. As they were driving together downtown, they passed the Ministry of Land Planning beside the bank of the Diyala River. The Iranians had blown it up several hours before, around noontime. Ibrahim looked at the mess and said, "Shit. I'm going to have to investigate that for the government." Adnan's early suspicions were accurate. Ibrahim's May 15 Organization was clearly working closely with the government. This became more evident as each day went by.

Adnan asked lots of questions, worried that he'd be caught. But Ibrahim said forged passports and visas were provided by the Iraqi government. "Don't worry, my friend," he reassured Adnan. "The Iraqi government and Abu Ibrahim protect each other." Even Rashid's brother, who Ibrahim said controlled a terrorist group in Lebanon, traveled with several passports; Ibrahim provided the brother with them so he could drive through Syria and Iraq. Adnan noticed Ibrahim kept a careful record of everything and had a specific file on Adnan. "He had to account for his expenses like any other legitimate business," Adnan said.

"He made me sign in my real name for the twenty thousand dollars he gave me and he made note of my alias so the government would know exactly who I was. He was very organized." Adnan was given two currencies: $15,000 in American money and $5,000 in Hungarian. Ibrahim, it appeared to Adnan, had been given a specific budget by the Iraqi government for a year's worth of terrorism. And like any government that gave money away, the Iraqi government demanded receipts and documentation of work completed.

The plan was for Adnan to travel to Geneva via Budapest under the name of Mohammed Jassin Khalaf. Anyone who spoke Arabic would know from Adnan's accent that he was not from the United Arab Emirates, as his passport claimed, but Ibrahim said there were no such officials to check on discrepancies like that. He wanted Adnan to stay for a week in Budapest, where he should spend money like a rich tourist. This would ensure that if anyone had followed him out of Baghdad, any suspicion that he was on a terrorist mission would be eliminated. After that he would fly to Zurich, then take the train to Geneva. If there was no room available at the Noga Hilton, Adnan was to stay somewhere close by and make a reservation as soon as a room was available.

His travel arrangements were placed in the capable hands of Mikhail, a twenty-five-year-old Lebanese man who assisted all May 15 members with their visas and passports. Mikhail told Adnan that he would initially fly to a communist country before going to Europe because the computers were not compatible and thus the trail of his flight pattern could not be traced.

He said the rewards of a successful mission would be fantastic. One standard guarantee was that the Iraqi government paid the rent for all of Ibrahim's people. They were also issued coupon books so they didn't ever have to purchase gas, and were given untraceable license-plate numbers.

Together, Mikhail and Adnan made the rounds of the embassies. Mikhail spoke several languages and seemed to know a lot of the diplomatic personnel. At the Italian embassy he filled out a visa application, despite Adnan's protests that he wasn't going to Italy. Mikhail explained that this was a precautionary measure. They liked to have visas to several countries in case anything went wrong. Next on the list was the Hungarian embassy, then they made a visit to the Swiss. It was only this last embassy that hesitated; they refused to give Adnan a visa unless he had a round-trip ticket. Ibrahim had made it perfectly clear that Adnan was not to come back to Baghdad directly from Geneva or anywhere else in Switzerland. Mikhail didn't have any worries. He'd dealt with red tape before and it was only a minor inconvenience. He bought the round trip, went back to the embassy for the visa, and then switched Adnan's return ticket.

It all seemed so easy. Adnan was shocked by the lack of security against would-be terrorists like himself. Mikhail said that he helped Ibrahim with missions all over the place and that terrorists actually would swap assignments—depending on who had easier access to a particular country. For instance, he said, Ibrahim had done a couple of missions for the German Baader-Meinhof group, allowing them to take the credit for his work because that made it easier for him to operate in Germany. In return, they would do missions for him in Israel. He had been told that even a faction of the Japanese Red Army had trained in a base in Baghdad for an operation planned against Jews in Israel.

Paranoia started to swell in the recesses of Adnan's mind. "Maybe," he thought, "there are a lot more terrorists in the world than I ever knew. Is it possible I just never noticed it before?" There'd be no escaping such a prolific international organization. Mikhail's parting words haunted him: "Be careful with Abu Ibrahim," he said. "If he doesn't like you, he'll send you on a one-way mission." *One-way mission.* The words rang in his ears. There was no mistaking the threat.

As the day for Adnan's departure grew closer, Ibrahim's instructions became more detailed. They returned to the locked room of the safe house and Adnan went over the plan. He asked if he would be stopped at the Iraqi airport. No, Ibrahim said. The security there would turn a blind eye by not examining his luggage. He would even enter a different door than all other passengers. The deal was that the detonator and the explosives had to be kept separate; they didn't want the whole world to start accusing the Arab countries of blatantly approving terrorism. The detonator would go in his shaving kit in the small carry-on bag. The explosive strips would be checked in the larger luggage.

Anyway, Ibrahim said, if you do get caught, just get in touch with the Iraqi ambassador in Switzerland. "You'll be set free," he said. "The Iraqi embassy in Switzerland works with us all the time."

Adnan was going along with Ibrahim's plan, not doing anything out of the ordinary that would betray his disloyalty. At this point, if he fell into disfavor, he knew too much to be discarded in a benign fashion. And anyway, even *before* he had been told the details of Ibrahim's operations, Ibrahim had made it clear he could easily destroy him. There weren't any options left for Adnan.

It was early August, and Rashid, about to leave on his mission, stopped by the safe house to say good-bye to Ibrahim while Adnan was there. Two months had passed from the time Adnan was introduced to Rashid by his old friend. Now he was about to embark on his own mission, a mission that he had never wanted in the first place. "Bad, stupid luck," he said. He chastised himself for not being more perceptive. From the start, his meeting with Rashid had been a carefully choreographed recruitment effort.

He never felt safe anymore. Even at night, in each other's arms, Ronac and Adnan spoke in hushed tones. Ibrahim had suggested that she go along on the mission, but Adnan didn't want her involved. He didn't eat much. He was nervous. She knew he was reluctant.

"I feel you're not coming back again," she said.

"Whatever happens will be for the best," Adnan told her.

He'd already made a decision, but he kept it to himself.

Early the next morning Adnan and Ronac stopped by Rashid's to say good-bye. They barely recognized him. He no longer had a mustache. His hair was cut very short and had been dyed blond.

Rashid said he went to the barbershop before every mission. Adnan felt compelled to ask something that had been lingering in his mind for some time now. He kept trying to get it out of his head, yet the more he tried to rid himself of the thought, the more he found himself obsessing over it. "How do you feel after you know somebody has died because of what you've done?" Adnan asked. As soon as the words left his mouth, Adnan berated himself for giving in to the temptation to ask such a question. It was a sign of weakness.

"The first mission I had trouble, but not after that," Rashid said. "Don't worry—you'll get used to it."

"Can it really be as simple as that?" Adnan wondered. "Will I really just 'get used to it'?" Where was the guilt, the feeling of remorse for killing someone, for taking someone's life? Adnan had felt guilty just *thinking* about the act of killing.

To Rashid, there were no feelings attached to his acts. He told Adnan that he had completed missions in Cairo and Istanbul and many in Europe, but he wouldn't say anything about where he was heading that day. It all seemed so carefree. It was as if he were going on a working vacation. Rashid didn't seem the slightest bit nervous, even though Fatima and their young son would be accompanying him. Rashid referred to Fatima as his "other passport" and laughed.

"Don't worry," he said. "We'll all meet back in Baghdad in three weeks."

4

Seat 47K

For Adnan's friend Mohammed Rashid, it would be a very busy working vacation indeed. Adnan learned of the details only much later.

At Baghdad International Airport, Mohammed Rashid, his wife, Fatima, and their three-year-old child looked like a picture-perfect European family on vacation, especially with Mohammed's slender build and dyed blond hair. But vacation was not exactly the object of their travels.

On July 15, 1982, Rashid and his wife had applied at the Japanese embassy for a visa to travel to Japan. When asked for his papers, he presented a photo of himself and a passport that showed his name to be Mohammed Harouk. Believing the credentials to be authentic, the embassy issued him a visa that same day in the name of Harouk, as well as visas for his wife and child, also under assumed names.

On or about August 7, the three flew to Singapore, where they'd cool their heels and act like tourists, as they had been instructed by Abu Ibrahim. At a Singapore travel agency, Rashid plunked down several thousand dollars in cash for the purchase of three Pan Am tickets to Hong Kong and Japan.

After three more days, Rashid and his family moved on to Hong Kong, where they stayed for two days. Then, on August 11, they boarded Pan Am Flight 002 for Tokyo. While his wife and child carried on as if they were typical tourists bound for Tokyo, Rashid went about his business. With his family serving as cover and lookout, Rashid took a small parcel no larger than a handbag from his carry-on baggage, carefully lifted the cushion of his seat, and wedged the bag into a totally obscured position.

Seat number 47K looked perfectly normal. And unless someone felt compelled to pry up the cushion, there would be no way of detecting the deadly cargo it now contained.

Mission accomplished, Rashid and his family disembarked at Narita Airport. They stayed in Tokyo forty-eight hours, then returned to Baghdad, retracing their steps along the same route.

As Rashid deplaned in Tokyo that day, August 11, he surely must have passed the Ozawa family from Sendai City as they checked in at Pan Am for their flight to Hawaii. They went to the same gate at which Flight 002 from Hong Kong had arrived. It was the same plane, aircraft number N754, that would take them to Honolulu for their long-sought vacation.

Sitting in seat 47K, adjacent to the window, was the fourteen-year-old teenager Toru. He was a high school junior. His parents, Shigetsu and Yoshko Oza, and his brother, Morikazu, sat in the same row to his left. His aunt and cousin were also sitting nearby.

Nearing the end of the long flight from Tokyo, 140 miles

from the Honolulu airport, the pilot announced that the Boeing 747 was beginning to its descent. Then a flight attendant read the perfunctory statement: "In preparation for the final approach to Honolulu Airport, passengers are kindly requested to pull their seat backs into the upright position and fasten their seat belts." It was 9:06 P.M. Flight 830's estimated time of arrival was 9:30.

On board were 267 passengers, 135 of them Japanese citizens, the rest American and other nationalities. It had been a typical Tokyo to Honolulu run, ferrying many tourists to the lush Pacific paradise. The chief flight attendant sounded the fasten-seat-belt chime.

As the flight attendants hurried down the aisles, checking seat backs and seat belts, the cabin's calm was shattered by a deafening explosion that had come from somewhere in economy class on the right side of the plane. The blast sent rained debris on everyone within forty feet as an acrid heavy blue smoke—the type caused by burning synthetics and plastic—filled the plane. A hole, one by three feet, was punctured in the wall separating the plane's cabin from the cargo hold, causing an immediate loss of pressure. In addition, a primary transverse I-beam support frame was fractured. At an altitude of thirty thousand feet, the plane started to drop like a rock. Since the plane continued to move forward, it was a "controlled fall," as the aircraft's despoilers choked off the airflow to reduce the airlift. But to passengers inside the cabin, it seemed as if the plane were literally falling out of the sky.

Pandemonium broke out, blood-curdling screams filling the cabin. As the plane dropped precipitously, there was not much one could do but pray. Some passengers donned life jackets, believing the plane would crash into the sea. Others sat motionless in their seats, frozen by fright.

"There was flying debris and then the whole area filled with smoke," Neil Lipper told the *Honolulu Star-Bulletin*. The smoke was so thick that passengers could not see the oxygen masks that were now dangling six inches in front of their faces.

The pilot, even with the cockpit beginning to fill with smoke, stopped the controlled fall at ten thousand feet—the altitude at which passengers can breathe without the help of oxygen masks—and managed to level off the plane. But the horror of the blast was just beginning to dawn on the passengers—especially those sitting in the economy class. Lying bloodied, mutilated, and with a hole in his stomach was a passenger, the passenger who had been sitting in seat 47K.

The force of the explosion had propelled Toru Ozawa into the air. One of his legs was blown off from the thigh down; a six-inch hole ripped through his abdomen. The blast was so close to his body that in the autopsy, medical examiners removed two inches of gold-plated nickel wire from one of his organs. The boy's mangled body ended up in the aisle, two feet away from his injured parents, who were bleeding profusely from their own injuries and splattered with the flesh and remains of their son. One could only imagine the horror and grief of Toru's parents, facing their dead son's unrecognizable body as they waited for the plane to land.

One minute he had been getting his bags ready for his vacation in Hawaii; the next, Toru lay in the plane, dead, his body virtually dismembered. Passenger Tom Stanton, fifteen feet away from the blast, recalled seeing Toru's maimed body lying in the aisle. An official coroner's report from the Honolulu Medical Examiner's Office would later conclude, using the antiseptic language reserved for medical reports, that Ozawa died from "traumatic injuries to the pelvis, abdomen, and right leg."

The plane finally landed at 9:28 P.M. at Honolulu Airport. Ambulances and fire trucks were waiting when the crippled airliner touched down. The injured passengers— including Toru's parents and twenty-six others—were strapped into ambulances. Toru's body, covered by a blanket, was carried off the plane by medical emergency workers. At 6:30 A.M. on the East coast, a spokesman for the Federal Aviation Administration released a statement saying that an incendiary device had been the cause of the explosion.

The FBI, FAA, and Honolulu police scoured the plane for clues and evidence. Every square inch of the cabin was dusted for explosive residue. Seat 47K, or what remained of it, and nearly two dozen other seats were removed for intensive laboratory analysis.

But there was not much known about what type of device it was, or who might have planted it. The Ozawa family, distraught and in shock, had to endure the painful intrusion of the FBI and the police questioning them about their travels, and, most painfully, the activities of their dead son. The FBI simply had no leads; in fact, the family was the only lead at the time—they were the victims and they also became the chief, though improbable, suspects.

Routine procedures required the investigators to examine the Ozawa family as possible suspects. Who were Toru's friends? Who packed their bags? Did the family have any enemies? Had Toru gotten mixed up in anything unusual in Japan? The questions were painful to ask, even more painful to answer. As expected, the interrogation produced no answers.

"Right now, we're totally in the dark," FBI Special Agent William C. Ervin, in charge of the Honolulu office, told reporters several days after the explosion.

Back in Japan, the National Police Academy initiated a major investigation into the cause of the explosion. They set up a special 105-man commission in the Narita Airport police station and arranged with the FBI to receive information on a full-time basis. Even before any of the FBI's preliminary interviews had been relayed to the academy, Japanese police investigators had begun to interview baggage handlers and other airport employees who had been in any kind of contact with the checked baggage.

By August 13, the FBI had come up with a set of tentative—and ultimately erroneous—findings. The bomb, they determined, had been placed around the right armrest of seat 47K—not under the seat, as initially thought. The investigators also believed that Toru may have brought the bomb onto the plane in his carry-on baggage. In fact, one FBI assessment stated that Toru had just leaned over to retrieve his hand baggage when the explosion took place. These judgments were conjectural rather than based on any hard forensic analysis; no part of the actual bomb was ever found and none of the micro remnants of the detonator were large enough to conduct any substantive analysis. A team of about fifty officials—from the Honolulu police, U.S. district attorney's office in Hawaii, Hawaii-based FBI, Washington, D.C., FBI headquarters, and the FAA continued to press forward with the investigation. A special FBI forensic and explosive team of experts, led by Denny Kline, the FBI's senior explosives expert, flew in from Washington.

The plane remained under guard at Honolulu Airport's Gate 20 as the FBI men set up a laboratory on it. After several days, the experts flew back to Washington, having packed a large cargo container with pieces of the plane and debris. The damaged 747 was flown back to New York a week later.

By August 15, having tentatively determined that the explosion was caused by nitroglycerin or dynamite and that it was definitely not an accident, the FBI sent word to the Japanese Police Academy to widen the scope of its investigation at Narita Airport. The bomb, they had concluded, must have been placed on board while the plane was on the ground at Narita or sometime prior to its arrival in Japan. Any stop made by the plane in the five days before the explosion had to be investigated. The 747 had left New York on August 8 and begun a round-the-world route, stopping off in London, Frankfurt, Istanbul, Riyadh, Bombay, Bangkok, Hong Kong, and finally, Tokyo, before heading for Honolulu. FBI and police officials began collecting lists of passengers who had boarded the plane at these previous stops, with a particular focus on Bangkok. Interviews had to be conducted all over the world.

Worldwide counterterrorist investigations were not something with which the FBI or Justice Department had much experience. They required hundreds of interviews—with passengers, baggage handlers, crew members, ticketing agents, cleaning crews. Investigators knew that *someone* had planted this bomb; finding that person amounted to a process of elimination. The only problem was that the universe of potential suspects numbered in the thousands. In fact, the investigation soon expanded to eight countries.

Still, what all detectives and crime solvers needed more than anything else was a motive. And in the bombing of Flight 830, there was not even a *hint* of a motive. It could have been an insurance scheme, a love triangle, a personal vendetta, even an attempted suicide. No one had claimed responsibility, which automatically ruled out the possibility that it was a political act. Some Japanese investigators initially thought the bombing could have been linked to radical Japanese protests that had beset Narita Airport. But that was quickly ruled out. The investigators were again left without a motive.

Even more frightening was the device's apparent level of sophistication. The bomb had been smuggled on board somehow, evading security devices at Narita. Despite its relatively small size, it had been powerful enough to rip a three-foot hole in the plane. To officials at the FAA, the explosive represented a quantum leap in bomb technology.

As investigators in the FBI's Washington headquarters continued to pore over evidence, they were alerted to the discovery of another bomb found on a Pan Am jet, this one in Brazil on August 25.

Flight 441 had just arrived in Rio de Janeiro from Miami. After the 210 passengers had disembarked, cleaning crews boarded the 747 jumbo jet to prepare it for the next flight. When they began vacuuming and throwing out garbage left behind on or under each seat, one of the crew members found a maroon vinyl bag, no larger than a small hand-held tote bag, under the window seat in row 29. This one had no name tag—and its position implied that someone had gone to extra lengths to wedge the bag under the cushion.

Given the high state of alert that American airlines—

particularly Pan Am—had been in since the bombing of the Honolulu-bound flight two weeks before, all crews were under strict instructions not to open or tamper with any unclaimed bags found on board flights. The cleaning crew immediately contacted the Brazilian federal police, who took possession of the bag.

At Rio police headquarters, explosives specialists determined the bag to be a bomb. Miraculously, it had failed to explode.

Walter Korsgaard, a retired lieutenant colonel and one of the government's most experienced explosives experts, was dispatched to Rio by Billy Vincent, director of the FAA's office of Civil Aviation Security. Korsgaard had been involved in the investigation of more than 150 bombs placed aboard airplanes. Brazilian authorities gave him and two bomb specialists from the FBI custody of the bomb, and they brought it back to the United States for analysis. Aboard a special FAA plane, they then transported it back to Washington to be dissected.

When told of the Brazilian bomb, Pan Am officials in New York were at first greatly relieved that it had not gone off. But that initial relief was replaced quickly with horror; some madman was apparently targeting the airline. This was the second bomb found on a Pan Am plane in two weeks. Was there a disgruntled employee? A terrorist group? Simply an insane individual? Why wasn't there any statement of responsibility? And why Pan Am?

These were the same questions being asked by the FBI and Japanese police officials. The pool of required interviews had now grown exponentially, as all passengers had to be checked out, including crew members and passengers who had boarded and exited the plane at previous stops. Flight 441 had originated in London, then flown to Miami and Rio. Somehow the bomb had evaded initial detection—and then on each leg of the trip, had been so well concealed that it had *again* eluded discovery.

It was now dawning on officials such as Billy Vincent that this anonymous bomb maker had perfected a device that could be smuggled anytime, in anything, and put onto a plane anywhere. And there was literally nothing that law-enforcement officials or airport security could do about it. Recalled Vincent, "We were absolutely dumb-founded by the bombs. They were made by someone who was not just a pro, but someone who was on the cutting edge of barometric bombs. It was not something we had seen before—and the problem was that we didn't know how we could stop the bomb maker from striking again." That sober acknowledgment was again impressed upon investigators a week or so later.

A third bomb was found, this one in Tokyo. Like the one in Rio, it had miraculously failed to explode, thereby averting the possible deaths of more than three hundred passengers. It was turned up by cleaning crews at Narita Airport after the plane had arrived from New York. The flight had originated in Frankfurt, and had stopped in London, then New York. Also like the bomb retrieved in Rio, this one had been found under a seat cushion. It was packed with the same type of plastic, wired with a baro-metric detonator.

Intelligence and law-enforcement officials from the United States and Japan decided to keep discovery of this latest bomb a secret, concerned that it would trigger worldwide panic. They also felt it imperative not to let the bomber know that the device had been found and was being analyzed for his "signature."

The most worrisome development was the realization that the person who had made the bomb had invented what FBI official Oliver "Buck" Revell would call a "near-invisible bomb." According to Vincent, "This level of sophistication and concealability had never been used in aviation before. Compared to previous known devices, these bombs were devastating."

The bombs were small enough to be concealed inside a man's suit-coat pocket, a woman's purse, a carry-on bag. The two AAA-size batteries that powered the bombs could be disguised in any number of legitimate electronic devices—radios and cassette players, for example,—routinely carried by passengers.

"There was a mass killer out there," recalled Noel Koch, a deputy assistant secretary of defense and head of the Pentagon's counterterrorism units. "He had the capability to destroy airplanes in midair at whim. It was only by the grace of God that [two of] the bombs we found had not gone off. We didn't know who or where this bomb maker was." For Koch at the Pentagon, Revell at the FBI, and others at the CIA, finding out the identity of the bomb maker before he succeeded in blowing up a plane in midair was their most urgent priority.

The investigation into the bombing of Pan Am Flight 830 and the placing of the bombs on the other flights required tight and close coordination among various intelligence and law-enforcement agencies, but each had its own interests to protect. The ensuing bureaucratic turf war slowed the investigation down. The CIA didn't want to disclose its sources to the FBI, nor did it want Justice Department lawyers breathing down its neck to make sure no corners were cut in looking for the bomber. The FBI didn't want to be forced to deal through the CIA and the fibbies certainly did not want to let go of possible witnesses deemed by the CIA too valuable to be exposed. That type of interagency friction was not abnormal; indeed, it was institutionally understandable and quite typical. The different U.S. government agencies were not used to cooperating with one another on intelligence investigations, particularly when the ultimate goal was to bring indictments. So while the forensic investigation proceeded rapidly, other aspects of the investigation lagged far behind.

Over the next few months, investigators finally made some headway in their examination of the thousands of passengers who had been aboard the flights to Honolulu, Rio, and Tokyo and on the more than fifteen legs of trips that preceded these final destinations.

One passenger in particular was looked at with great interest: the man who sat in seat 47K on Flight 002 from Hong Kong to Tokyo on August 11. From the passenger manifest and the Pan Am computers, investigators plucked his name: Mohammed Harouk. He apparently lived in Iraq. He had gotten off in Tokyo, stayed two days, then left. The last airline computer entry showed that he returned to Baghdad via Singapore.

Then investigators found something extraordinary. The same Mohammed Harouk had traveled to Europe, where he boarded another Pan Am flight that went on to London. From Heathrow the flight went to Miami and then to Rio de Janeiro—where the cleaning crews had found the lethal maroon vinyl bag. Mohammed Harouk was clearly the person investigators wanted and needed to interview. Japanese investigators asked their embassy in Baghdad to provide them with a copy of the visa application that Harouk had filled out. The information was immediately forwarded to the CIA and FBI.

An initial search of Western counterterrorist data bases failed to generate any information about Mohammed Harouk. Further investigation showed several discrepancies on the visa application, particularly one egregious and problematic one: Mr. Mohammed Harouk did not exist.

5

Geneva and the Bomb

Now it was Adnan's turn. On August 8, 1982, Ronac and Mikhail drove him to the Baghdad International Airport just eleven miles north of the city.

He was wearing a brown suit with a beige silk shirt, Bally leather shoes, an Omega watch, and a diamond ring. Slung over his shoulder was a large tan garment bag. It had a bomb sewn into its seams.

Adnan was petrified. Even though Ibrahim had assured him of the government's full knowledge of and cooperation with May 15 missions, Adnan imagined security officials arresting him before he ever got near the plane. Then he would spend the rest of his life in a tough Iraqi jail. Mikhail made fun of his insecurity and took him through a back door at the terminal, bypassing Iraqi security inspections altogether. This was routine. Abu Ibrahim had arranged for all his operatives to smuggle bombs onto planes via a secret agreement with the government.

Once inside the terminal, Mikhail shouted to airport security-officer friends, who in turn waved hello. They smiled at him as he made a face, pointing to the bag

Adnan was holding. Then Mikhail motioned with his hands how delicate the bag was, pantomiming the effects of an explosion. Adnan was flabbergasted. It was like one of the Jerry Lewis movies he so enjoyed. It was unreal. Yet it was clear to him that Mikhail had done this many times before. The guards laughed and wished Adnan godspeed. "It cannot be this easy," Adnan said to himself. But it was. Adnan had absolutely no trouble checking the large tan garment bag with the bomb in it. No one even looked at it. For a split second, Adnan worried that if no one searched his bag, countless other passengers could have brought bombs on board too. Was it possible that the plane would be blown up by another bomb?

Saying good-bye to Ronac at the gate was devastating. He had been able to confide in her. She was the only one who knew his misfortune—the sole comfort amid the horrid circumstances that were rapidly shaping his future. Now he would be alone. Even worse, Abu Ibrahim had become his keeper.

Adnan's flight departed at II P.M. As he boarded the plane, he glanced around the cabin at the other passengers. Mostly families on vacation, they were excited about their European destination. They laughed and told stories in the same excited way that all people do when they go on airplane trips.

His head felt heavy. He was depressed. He could feel the other passengers' thoughts even though their lips were sealed: "What's wrong with this guy? Why isn't he happy?"

Adnan was dying to explain.

During the course of the seven-hour flight, Adnan thought of every possible scenario. If the government caught him, he reasoned, that would be good. It wouldn't look as though he had squealed. It wouldn't be his fault. Maybe he'd be arrested, the bomb would be confiscated, and he could call the Iraqi ambassador, who would set him free. He looked around at all the happy passengers. It was like a nightmare that was all the more frightening because it was so real. How could everyone be so happy, he thought, when he was hopelessly stuck in a situation that spelled disaster for him?

As the plane was about to land in Budapest, Adnan sincerely hoped that in the customs or immigration search, his bomb would be discovered. But when he arrived the security people were very nice. They opened his luggage, poking here and there, but never where he wanted them to. They cleared him, smiling all the time and wishing him a pleasant stay in the city.

He spent the next ten days trying to spend his money like a rich man with no cares, and certainly no bomb on his mind. He thought to himself that he wasn't much good at pretending.

The bomb was omnipresent. Its existence was so nerve-wracking Adnan could hardly stand being in his hotel room. He hated changing his clothes because it meant dealing with his suitcase and once again feeling the wave of panic his secret cargo elicited.

"I was so sad I didn't know what I was doing from moment to moment," he said. "I lost track of time. I couldn't even remember if I had eaten or not."

Even though his army days had taught him that there was no way the bomb could go off without first being set up, he obsessively worried that the chambermaid would light a cigarette or somehow trigger the explosives while she was cleaning his room.

When he wasn't thinking about the bomb prematurely exploding, he tried to imagine aborting his mission and escaping the revenge of Ibrahim. But he convinced himself not to tell anyone just yet about his orders, and, afraid Ibrahim had someone watching him, he remained in Budapest for the exact amount of time that Ibrahim had advised. He acted like a tourist, avoided all political magazines, and minded his own business. Then he bought his ticket to Zurich according to plan.

When his plane touched down in Switzerland in late August 1982, he said a prayer: "Thank you, God, for sending me to Switzerland: a place that will not tolerate terrorism."

There was a line at customs.

Up ahead, Adnan saw a hippie who was suddenly pulled aside.

"They got him; they'll surely get me," he thought. *"Please* find my bomb." He was certain that now he would be saved from having to carry out his mission.

When the security people opened Adnan's luggage, he was immediately relieved. They asked if he had anything to claim. He said no, expecting that they wouldn't believe him and would investigate further. Instead, they told him to enjoy his stay.

In less than a second, all of Adnan's hopes had been dashed. He had reached the country of his bomb's destination. Ibrahim was right: Nobody could find his invisible bomb. He couldn't get caught no matter how hard he tried.

He took a taxi to the train station and the train from Zurich to Geneva. When he arrived, he went straight to the Noga Hilton on the edge of Lake Geneva. The hotel was colossal. Besides its 316 guest rooms, the Noga had a reputation for hosting large international seminars and conferences. The hotel had a grand casino, discotheques, bars, gaming rooms, a shopping gallery, and restaurants. It looked like a separate city.

Ibrahim had told Adnan to try to get a room on a middle floor of the hotel so that the whole thing would collapse like a tower of cards. Ibrahim had studied the layout of the hotel, based on the surveillance of an earlier courier, who had taken photos of the Noga Hilton and drawn a diagram.

As he walked into the lobby, Adnan was amazed by the accuracy of Ibrahim's description. It looked exactly how it was supposed to look.

Ibrahim had even given very specific instructions on how he was to go about checking in. "The clerks," he had said, "may be suspicious of you because the owner does not trust Arabs. When you ask for a room, give him your passport at the same time. Don't give him a chance to say no."

Adnan walked to the registration counter, where a young man with dark hair and fair skin told him the hotel was full. He could make a reservation for three days from that day if he wanted. The news brought a smile to Adnan's face, much as he tried to suppress it and feign disappointment to the hotel clerk. Adnan asked him where the nearest hotel was. Down the street, he was told, just a few blocks away.

As Ibrahim had instructed, he went to the hotel down the street and booked a room. He followed this contingency plan to the letter, again fearing that somebody was watching to make sure he did as Ibrahim had commanded.

He knew it was paranoia, but Adnan almost sensed a pair of eyes staring at him as he signed the register at the second hotel.

When he got to his room, he started debating with himself. Maybe he would speak with the owner of the hotel and explain the whole story? Maybe he wouldn't. Who would believe him? He hardly believed it himself.

By day Adnan spent his time at the Noga. There was plenty to do there. It was just as he imagined it was in Las Vegas. The only time he had ever heard of Las Vegas was in an old Martin and Lewis movie. Adnan met an Iraqi doctor in his fifties and they played roulette. Adnan stuck to his story but the doctor immediately saw through it.

"You are not from the United Arab Emirates," he said.

Adnan explained that he was a Palestinian who later got a passport. Adnan was hoping he would be discovered. Ibrahim had warned him about speaking to other Arabs who would quickly pick up regional accents and could later contradict his alibi.

But the doctor said only, "This is baloney, but this is also not my business."

The next day, Adnan sat outside on the deck overlooking the lake. A young woman invited him to sit with her and they talked most of the afternoon. "I knew what was on her mind, but nothing except the bomb was on mine," Adnan said. She asked him to call her. He knew he wouldn't.

A few days later he returned to the Noga Hilton to confirm his reservation. Everything was fine, the clerk said. His room was available. But, in a spur-of-the-moment decision, Adnan canceled the reservation. The clerk seemed puzzled but was in no position to question him. Having abruptly decided to remain in the hotel he had been staying at, Adnan returned there only to learn they had booked his room. He now had to go to a third hotel in the area.

Adnan was talking to himself more and more. Sometimes he would catch himself at it and then yell at himself. He looked in the mirror at times, talking to his image as if he were outside his own body. His rantings would overwhelm him at inexplicable moments. He was overtired and hungry but too nauseous to eat. Just as he had feared in Budapest, he wondered whether the bomb was going to go off in Switzerland before he did anything with it.

He put the bomb on his new bed, feeling a surge of panic. He realized he was becoming hysterical but he couldn't stop himself from talking out loud—pleading with this bomb that had consumed his life. "Why don't you kill me now?" he asked. "Why don't you let me die?"

His nerves were frayed. He felt he was going crazy. "Is this what crazy people go through?" he wondered. How much longer could he take this? Every minute felt like an eternity. He could almost hear the clock ticking in his head. He jumped at the sound of police or ambulance sirens. One moment he felt relieved, the next he was completely helpless. He was desperate. Maybe he should have married Selma, lived in Damascus, and had too many kids.

He was not going through with the attack. He'd actually known he wouldn't all along, he told himself. But how would he get rid of the bomb?

He had to warn somebody about it. Maybe an airline would help him. He remembered Ibrahim repeatedly saying he wanted to target Pan Am because it was a symbol of the United States. Adnan had asked why other American airlines wouldn't be just as good. Ibrahim told him that other American airlines, such as TWA, meant nothing to Arabs—they didn't understand what the initials represented. For all they knew it could be a French airline. He wanted his message to be clear: Anyone that was a friend of Israel was an enemy of the Arab nations.

Suddenly, Adnan felt certain that if he told Pan Am his secret, they would help him out. He found the Pan Am office in Geneva; it was a five-minute walk from his hotel. He asked for the manager, but he was on vacation. The receptionist asked if she could help. Adnan shook his head. He needed to speak to someone in authority. The receptionist said she could handle anything he needed. Was it a matter of changing a reservation or getting a refund? she wanted to know. No! Adnan responded. It was nothing—nothing at all.

He went back to his room. He was at the breaking point, his nerves tattered.

"Think, think, think!" he said aloud. "What can I do?"

He began laying out his possible options. If he went to Syria, he worried that they wouldn't like him for squealing. If he went to the Israeli ambassador, Adnan's name would get in the paper and Ibrahim would kill him. And going to the American embassy would be the same as going to the Israelis, at least as far as Ibrahim was concerned. Finally he came up with a solution. He would go to the Saudi Arabian consulate. The Saudis, he thought, were friends with Americans *and* Arabs.

"I felt like Archimedes," he said. *"Wagtoha!"**

For the first time in a fortnight, he began to relax. He told himself that everything was going to be all right. The

*An Arabic expression meaning "Eureka!"

next morning he went to the Saudi consulate on Rue Maunoir.

Mohmoud el-Shafii, the consul's special assistant, shook his hand. He told Adnan that the consul was at a meeting out of town. Was there something he could help him with?

Adnan nervously pulled his passport from his breast pocket and handed it to Shafii.

"What do you think of it?" he asked.

"There's nothing wrong with this passport," the assistant said. "But you are not from this country."

Adnan told him that he was right and asked if he would meet him at the Noga hotel that afternoon after work. He said it was very important. Shafii was puzzled and said that his time was very important. Couldn't they discuss what he wanted to talk about right there and then? No, said Adnan, realizing that he wasn't yet prepared to blurt out his terrible secret. His plan was to meet Shafii at the Noga Hilton—then take him back to his hotel and show him the bomb.

Shafii arrived exactly on time. Adnan was so anxious he'd gotten there two hours earlier. He wondered if the police would be accompanying the stranger he'd confided in at the consulate.

Instead, Shafii was alone. They sat down in a discreet corner. An Arab couple had just gotten married and there were many people milling about the lobby. They walked past Adnan and Shafii as if on cue.

"What would you think if all these people were to die and this entire hotel came crashing down?" Adnan asked.

Shafii was completely taken off guard and wanted to know what Adnan could possibly be talking about.

"This is my mission," he said. "I've been sent by

Abu Ibrahim of Iraqi to kill these people."

Shafii looked aghast. "Please talk quietly," he said. "What are you saying? This is very serious—you should not joke."

"I am very serious," Adnan responded. "I am here to kill these people."

Adnan felt grateful that at least Shafii did not think he was crazy. He tried to speak slowly and rationally, even though he would have preferred to stand up and scream.

"Come to the consulate tomorrow morning," Shafii said. "I will try to reach the consul." He looked very worried—which was not very reassuring to Adnan.

It was a sleepless night for Adnan. He kept wondering whether he'd done the right thing, wondering whether the Saudi diplomat would betray him. He wondered whether there would be a knock on his door at any time or whether he would be shot while he slept. These thoughts tormented him the entire night.

Adnan got up at five o'clock the next morning. Too nervous to eat, he just sat staring at the bomb. At nine he arrived at the Saudi consulate, where Shafii was waiting. Adnan could already read the expression on his face. He seemed disappointed and agitated at the same time.

"I hate to tell you this," Shafii said. "But the consul does not want to get involved. I'm sorry. He'd like you to leave immediately."

Adnan was shocked. "What do you mean he doesn't want to see me? I have a bomb! He *must* see me!"

But Shafii wasn't budging. "You must leave now. There is nothing we can do for you. We do not want to get mixed up in this affair. I am sorry, but you must leave right now."

Adnan could hardly believe what he was hearing and walked out, bitterly disappointed. He had pinned his hopes on the Saudis. But his disappointment soon turned to anger. Shouldn't they have at least arrested him for possessing a false passport? The moment he left the consulate, he got scared. The Saudis were incapable of taking a stand on Palestinian terrorism. If they couldn't or wouldn't openly oppose it, maybe they, too, condoned it.

"What if they betray me to the Iraqi government?" he thought. "Maybe they're already working in conjunction with Ibrahim. Maybe I'm under surveillance right now." Adnan looked all around him but there was no one watching.

Adnan had never been a compliant person. He'd always had trouble with authority and didn't like taking orders. So why was he doing it now?

Because the alternatives were few. He could detonate the bomb and return to Iraqi a celebrity. He could call Ibrahim and say that he couldn't go through with the mission. He figured that option would most likely result in death by torture. Or he could tell his story to a country that found terrorism reprehensible. (As the Saudis had proved, going to his own people was useless.)

There was only one way out. He could turn the tables on the situation. He could be a hero in the true sense of the word rather than the warped Iraqi definition. He could save hundreds of lives—not destroy them. He could turn himself in to the people who suspected Palestinians almost as much as the Israelis did, and bargain that they'd treat him fairly.

"To hell with it," he said as he walked along the street. "I'm going to the American embassy."

It was an impulsive decision that Adnan didn't have time to consider. Had he thought about it, he might have changed his mind.

He jumped in a taxi. "Take me immediately to the American embassy!" he shouted at the driver, who looked at him as though he were out of his mind.

"There is no American embassy in Geneva," he said dryly. "You'll have to go to Bern—it's a long and expensive fare."

Adnan made a decision: He would never come back to Geneva; he would never see the bomb he left under his bed in his hotel room again. He told the cab driver to take him to Bern.

"Whatever happens is in God's hands," he told himself. "I don't care. I no longer live with a bomb."

He arrived at the American embassy in Bern, on Jubilaeumsstrasse, at closing time, Tuesday, August 31. The taxi screeched to a halt in front of the entrance and, panicked, the security guards jumped into action.

"Move the taxi, move the taxi," they said, flailing their arms, fearing a car bomb would obliterate their piece of democracy abroad.

Adnan was shaken. "If a superpower is so scared about terrorism what will they do to me when I confess?" he wondered.

The taxi pulled away and Adnan walked up the steps of the embassy. There were security cameras everywhere and the three beefy policemen on guard outside the white stone rectangular building toted machine guns. The embassy was close to the Aare, the main river flowing through Bern, in a serene residential district. The guards looked extremely officious and their pressed uniforms and deadpan expressions reminded Adnan of all the American movies he'd watched in Damascus.

They glanced at him sideways, making it obvious it wasn't too often that Arabs entered their domain. They were already suspicious.

Inside, two more guards in fancier military dress stood by as Adnan walked through a metal detector. He then went up to a Plexiglas window and told an older woman that he needed to speak with an official.

Ten minutes later Adnan met his first American. The diplomat was about forty-five years old and was wearing a conservative dark suit. He was nearly six feet tall and his hair and mustache were silver with flecks of black. His face was very serious.

He asked Adnan what he could help him with. Adnan told him he had something important to speak about and was there a safe place that they could be alone. The diplomat could tell Adnan was anxiety-ridden. They stepped in an elevator and went up a few floors. Once upstairs, the diplomat unlocked the door to a light-gray medium-sized room with bars on its windows. The furniture was sparse—just a table and chairs. It was not relaxing, but it was secure.

"I have a bomb," Adnan said. "I've been sent to blow up the Geneva Noga Hilton hotel."

He was numb. He'd gone over his story so many times that now, as he repeated it finally to someone who would listen and actually do something about it, it didn't seem real. For a second after he finished speaking, a feeling of total paranoia came over Adnan. Maybe they, too, were working with the Iraqis, he thought to himself.

Adnan gave the diplomat the address and phone number where he had been staying in Geneva. Saying he was going to pass the information along to the Swiss police, the diplomat left the room. When he returned, he mildly interrogated Adnan, asking him how long he had been in Switzerland and where he had come from.

The unburdening of his secret had exhausted Adnan, making it even more of a struggle than usual for him to communicate in a language he seldom used. Half an hour went by before a woman came in, speaking rapid-fire German to the diplomat. The muscles in the diplomat's face tensed as he heard the news, and he then turned to Adnan.

"Why are you lying to me?" he demanded. "We've emptied an entire hotel. We've frightened people." Neither the Swiss police, he said, nor their bomb-sniffing dogs had found any explosives in Adnan's room. The diplomat accused Adnan of trying to avoid paying his hotel bill. There were many reactions Adnan had anticipated, but this was certainly not one of them. His trepidation suddenly turned to anger. His pride had been hurt and his integrity called into question.

"I'm not lying! I'm not crazy!" Adnan screamed back.

"Why did you come here?" the diplomat yelled. "What is it you want?"

Adnan could hardly believe he was now in a shouting match with the American. "There is a bomb in my hotel room," he insisted. "Let's go there together and if I'm lying, kill me."

The diplomat stopped his tirade and asked Adnan to draw a diagram of exactly where the bomb was located and what it looked like. Adnan made a quick sketch of the luggage, indicating the seams that had to be separated to reveal the explosives. The diplomat picked up the phone, quickly spouted off the latest information, and hung up.

Then they waited. And waited. They mostly just stared at each other while the American blew smoke rings. When the phone finally rang ten minutes later—ten minutes that seemed an eternity to Adnan—it was like an alarm clock striking loudly in the middle of a deep sleep for him. He jumped back in his chair.

The diplomat answered, listened for a few seconds, then smiled. Adnan realized the bomb had been found. As soon as he got off the phone the American offered Adnan a drink.

The diplomat spent two more hours with the Palestinian, asking specifically how Adnan had gotten involved with Ibrahim. He said that Adnan was safe now and that in the morning he would like to speak with him again.

It was late and far past the embassy's closing hour. He opened his wallet to give the "reluctant bomber" some money for a hotel.

"I don't want your money," Adnan said. "I want to get rid of a bomb."

That night when he ordered dinner, he was able to enjoy food for the first time in weeks. He felt giddy. He laughed and indulged in his most recent habit of talking to himself out loud.

"Whatever happens to me," he said, "at least there's no more invisible bomb."

During the entire ordeal, Adnan had never once considered that he might be thrown in jail or treated miserably for being an accomplice in a killer's scheme. His primary thought was to physically get rid of the bomb. Not once did he think of what the consequences of turning himself in would be. Now he began to wonder.

The next morning at eight o'clock he returned to the American embassy. The diplomat he had met the night before was waiting for him. He thanked Adnan profusely but explained that he must let the Swiss police handle the matter because it was their jurisdiction by law.

Adnan said that before anything else transpired he would need a translator. "Someone who can speak Arabic," he requested, "but is not Arab." He still was acutely aware of the danger he was in and did not want an Arab—who could be a double agent—reporting to the Iraqi government on Adnan's confession. There would surely be retribution.

An hour later, the diplomat and Adnan walked outside of the American embassy, where the Swiss federal police were waiting. He was introduced to Captain Michelle and a translator named Max.

Max's Arabic was so good that Adnan was certain he was an Arab, even though he was fair and had blond hair. He got angry, but Max pulled out his Swiss passport and explained that while he had worked with Arab diplomats for thirteen years he was Swiss and was working solely for them.

The American diplomat said that the ambassador, Faith Whittlesey, would check in on him. The Swiss opened the back door of a BMW and Max said, "Don't be scared."

They drove Adnan to the Swiss federal court, where he repeated his entire story. He went over his descriptions of Rashid and Ibrahim. He described the safe houses that Ibrahim had used throughout Baghdad and the level of support the Iraqi government had provided Ibrahim. He explained how Ibrahim had made the bombs and described the makeshift laboratory where the suitcase bombs were manufactured. For Adnan, spilling his guts felt good, yet it was also unnerving. Was he betraying his people? he asked himself. What about his family? What about Ronac? What about his friends? These were questions he had not stopped to consider. But now it was too late. There was no going back.

The Swiss placed Adnan in protective custody in a safe house outside of the city and had him make a list of the foods he liked to eat. In the morning he'd return to Bern.

"Every day there were questions, questions, questions," Adnan remembers. Meanwhile, they were debriefing him, methodically verifying his story to make sure he was telling the truth and was not a double agent. They gave him maps of Baghdad and asked him to identify where his sister lived and where his business was located.

The Swiss authorities were incredibly thorough. They presented Adnan with a sheet of paper, sitting across the table from him with another piece of paper before them. They went down a long list of inquiries. For each answer Adnan gave them, they would cross-reference. Swiss officials later said that Adnan's story corresponded with their intelligence.

"Now we are sure your story is all right," Captain Michelle said finally. "What can we do for you?"

"I don't want my name, photograph, or any mention of this in the newspapers," Adnan said, knowing full well that Ibrahim would be able to find him if that occurred. He didn't want even to think about what would happen if it did. The Swiss agreed.

They said that they were willing to bring Ronac to Switzerland, but Adnan knew his future was unstable and didn't want to subject her to an insecure situation. Although his business would have to be sacrificed, Adnan had a huge amount of savings. He asked the Swiss to withdraw his money and gave them all the information about his accounts.

A week later Swiss intelligence had news: The Iraqi government had taken everything. They had seized all the money in his accounts, all of his cars, and his home, and would not cash the last check he'd written to Ronac, as a precaution if he should not return.

"It was as I expected," Adnan recalled. "Ibrahim and the government were efficiently working together."

The Swiss were extremely understanding. "You made a very good decision and you've helped us," Captain Michelle said. They gave him a BMW, a salary of $700 a week, and a Swiss passport, and told him he could live in Switzerland as long as he liked. He found an apartment in Bern.

In return, Adnan gladly helped the Swiss. "They sat down with me and we discussed how to prevent terrorism," he said. Among their primary concerns was how to stop people from getting visas to places they were not supposed to go.

"I told them that all the rules should be uniform," Adnan said. "And that the round-trip airline ticket that is needed to obtain the visa must never be allowed to be changed."

He also thought that there should be an Arabic-speaker in each Swiss embassy so that any Arab terrorist coming in with a false passport and requesting a visa could easily be identified if his accent did not match the country he claimed to be from.

The Swiss arranged a large meeting between Adnan and foreign intelligence services, including agents from the

CIA, the British MI-6, the French Deuxième Bureau, and the Mossad.

Officials from the FBI, CIA, Justice Department, and Defense Department were given briefings based on the information supplied by Adnan. But the briefings were not very extensive. The only conclusive result was that now, for the first time, U.S. law-enforcement officials had a name and an address for the person who had been behind the attempted mass terrorism that nearly succeeded in destroying three airplanes: Abu Ibrahim.

"He's called the Bomb Man, or the Bomb Maker, in Arabic. He's known throughout the radical Palestinian terrorist element as the most proficient bomb maker," recalled Buck Revell.

The Americans came with pictures of suspected Palestinian terrorists and concealed bombs and weapons. Leading the delegation was a Justice Department official named Daniel Bent, at that time the assistant U.S. attorney in Hawaii. Bent was particularly interested in finding out who had placed the bomb on Flight 830 to Hawaii.

According to Adnan, he had close to fifty photographs and asked if Adnan could identify Mohammed Rashid. Adnan did. He also found photographs of Fatima, Zuhair, Abdul Razzak el-Nashashibi, and other terrorists he had come into contact with. Included in that group was Nashashibi's cousin Marwan—the spy in Israel—whom Adnan had met a couple of times. Shortly after Adnan's identification, Adnan was told the Mossad had arrested Marwan.

Adnan was repeatedly gripped with mixed and ambivalent feelings about what he was doing. He knew without a doubt that he was repelled by terrorism, but beyond giving up the bomb, should he be revealing the secrets of other people who had trusted him? Adnan grappled with this personal dilemma, unsure if he was doing the right thing.

As the weeks passed and Adnan became more familiar with intelligence experts, he became more convinced that what he was doing *was* the right thing. Perhaps it was because there was no reminder of his home or his friends anymore. He realized he was cut off from everyone he had ever known. Strangely, he felt no twinges of loneliness. That would come later.

While all of Adnan's information was extraordinarily helpful to Western intelligence officials, one of the most important tips he gave was a detailed description of Abu Ibrahim. The CIA and other intelligence groups had no idea what the man behind such successful terrorist acts even looked like. Adnan described Ibrahim in minute detail, from the color of his eyes to the slight scar he had on his elbow. He described Ibrahim's strong personality, his ability to get his own way. At the same time, Adnan told the intelligence officials, Ibrahim was a personally cautious man, not at all like Mohammed Rashid, who reveled in his self-importance and his material possessions.

But the Mossad wasn't entirely satisfied. Of all the intelligence agencies, they were the only one to bring an Arabic-speaking agent. Asking to speak with Adnan privately, they brought in a lie-detector machine and asked him if he would mind being hooked up to it. Adnan said okay. The two Mossad agents hooked him up. "Have you killed anyone?" and "Was this your first mission?" were among their questions. It wasn't until he passed this test that the Mossad was convinced of his authenticity.

So convinced, in fact, that they asked him to become a

double agent for them. They wanted him to go to Paris and live the life of a rich Arab while maintaining his contacts with Palestinian terrorists. In return, they would pay him $5 million, depositing the money in a Swiss account.

They promised that they could create a bombing in the Noga Hilton so that Ibrahim would think he had ultimately carried out the mission and said there'd even be a report of injuries. It was the first time he had ever met someone from the Mossad. All he knew was what he was told in the Arab world—that the Mossad killed anyone they didn't like and that they had spies everywhere. Mossad people, he had imagined, were not human. Abu Ibrahim and Rashid had constantly talked about being hunted by the Mossad.

But Adnan came away feeling impressed with the Israelis. He saw for the first time that his longtime enemies were very human and seemed concerned about his welfare, and he understood why they were so good at what they did. He even appreciated the Israelis' fears of terrorism.

He was tempted by their offer, but he knew that what he had done up until then—giving up and providing intelligence on Ibrahim and Rashid—was the most he could do. He could not completely turn around and begin working for his former enemy—the very people he had been assigned to kill. "I knew that once the Israelis find terrorists, they have to kill them—and I could not do that to my people," he said.

"I turned them down. I told them that I didn't want to go back into the terrorism business and that if I had any desire to get back into it, I would have done it for my own people."

6

The Signature

A continent away, investigators were getting their first look at the handiwork of the "master bomb maker." Denny Kline at FBI headquarters in Washington was the point man. And he was preoccupied with one thing: the signature.

To handwriting experts, a signature tells a lot about a person's identity. Loops and squiggles betray facets of one's personality. Similarly, to explosives experts, the way a bomb is devised is the single most important evidence in determining its maker's identity.

By looking at its construction, it is possible to retrace the building of a bomb piece by piece. The plastic explosives, the detonator, the wiring, the timer, even the container in which the bomb was built, are all clues.

Kline was America's bomb supersleuth. When he joined the FBI in 1969, he was assigned to the Newark field office, where he worked on bombings carried out by Omega 2 (the anti-Castro Cuban resistance), the Puerto Rican FALN resistance, and the Weathermen, the radical U.S. student group. In 1976, Kline was transferred to the explosives laboratory, where he became the chief expert.

Much as a surgeon is called in the middle of the night to rush to the hospital for emergency surgery, Kline had been notified of the explosion on board Pan Am Flight 830. It was time to operate.

He left immediately for Honolulu, where he supervised the retrieval, handling, and processing of the exploded areas inside the plane. After intensive analysis, Kline and other investigators concluded that the explosive device was probably something called pentaerythritol tetranitrate (known as PETN), an explosive used in the manufacture of detonators, blasting caps, and Semtex, a powerful plastic explosive manufactured by Czechoslovakia. Kline knew something about PETN. It was a white crystalline substance usually sold in large quantities to military forces. From the analysis of the explosive residue on Pan Am 830, it appeared to Kline that the PETN used was a "homemade mixture," and that it had probably been prepared in sheet form.

Also among the debris were two AAA-size 1.5-volt batteries. On one of them the manufacturer's printed code could be discerned as "081." A two-inch piece of gold-plated nickel wire was removed from Toru Ozawa's body. It was 24-karat and thirty thousandths of an inch thick.

Kline was still working on the tedious analysis, sifting through all the materials and running tests, when he got a call from the FBI operations center. A bomb, he was told, had just been retrieved from a Pan Am jet in Rio de Janeiro. The Rio police bomb squad had safely transported the bomb to its laboratory, where it was dismantled.

Kline joined Walter Korsgaard and other officials in Rio and flew the bombs back to Washington on an FAA executive jet—commercial airlines understandably didn't want bombs being transported on their aircraft, even if they were disconnected. But on the way back, the FAA jet lost power in two of its engines over the United States. For several moments, it seemed as if the plane would not make it. It was almost like a joke, Kline thought, being killed in a crash due to engine malfunction when he was carrying a bomb aboard. Radioing a Mayday, the pilot made an emergency landing in Charleston.

Once safely back at FBI headquarters, Kline was anxious to begin dissecting the bomb. It was an unprecedented opportunity to analyze the bomber's signature intact. Most of his work involved bombs that had already been detonated.

This was a bomb the likes of which he had never seen. Wrapped in a maroon vinyl covering that had apparently been cut from a piece of luggage, it weighed three quarters of a pound. According to his analysis, the bomb itself was to be triggered by a "subminiature audio jack, an improvised direct pressure switch, an E-Cell time-delay circuit encased in an epoxy potting material, and an electric detonator." A chemical analysis of the explosive material found that it consisted of a "mixture of 80 percent PETN and 20 percent rubber latex adhesive binder wrapped in a cheesecloth-type material."

The two batteries were AAA 1.5-volt and had been "secured with black plastic tape and connected together with wire, copper tabs, and a battery snap connector." Significantly, the manufacturer's codes on the batteries read "08r"—the same as those in the Honolulu bomb. On the explosive itself, there was handwriting from a blue ballpoint pen. The numbers "7.30" had been written in both Farsi and Arabic—this indicated "the amount of time delay that the bomb was set for," Kline reported.

Further analysis of the Rio bomb proved even more significant. According to Kline's analysis, the "time-delay electric circuit consisted of an E-Cell, 12k ohm resistor and transistor." The E-Cell, an electrochemical timer, noted the report, "bore the printing 'Plessey, U.S.A. 560-0002.'" An examination of the E-Cell revealed that its two electrode wires were "made of gold-plated nickel wire" and that the plating was "24-karat and the thickness thirty thousandths of an inch"—identical to the segment retrieved from Toru's body.

Kline also noted the way in which the bomb was to be detonated: "The direct pressure switch was made from a plastic disc which had been machine ground to form a hollow core. A rubber membrane was secured over the open end of the disc. Copper contacts were inserted on the inside of the rubber membrane and through the plastic disc. When the rubber membrane is depressed the two contacts come together and allow for the flow of current to the E-Cell time-delay circuit. The subminiature jack is used as an arming switch along with the connection of the battery power source into the electrical circuit. A plastic plunger was found inside the jack, which had been broken on one end. The plunger was stuck in the jack with adhesive and suggests that the plunger was broken in an attempt to remove it from the jack when arming the device."

The bomb's functions were quite simple. First the battery power had to be connected. Then the plastic plunger had to be removed from the subminiature jack to "arm the electrical circuit." Then the bomb had to be placed under the seat. When a passenger sat on it, the pressure would activate the E-Cell time delay. In turn, the E-Cell would send out currents and direct it to the detonator, which then would trigger the bomb.

Had the bomb gone off, it would have, at a minimum, killed several passengers; if it punctured the cabin skin at a high enough altitude, the plane could have exploded in midair, killing everyone on board.

The bomb was a diabolically clever device. According to FAA official Billy Vincent, "The barometric sensor served as a switch, which activated the bomb when it was flown above a certain altitude. When the aircraft descended below this altitude, the bomb would become inactive, though time might still be remaining in the E-Cell timer. When the bomb was again carried above the predetermined altitude, the barometric sensor would activate the timing system again. This sequence would repeat itself until the timer expired, and then the bomb would explode. The timing and barometric sensing system guaranteed that the device would only explode while the airplane was flying."

At the FBI, Kline decided to replicate the bombs and their explosions—in order to test their explosive impact and see whether the anticipated blast would be similar to the explosion that killed Toru Ozawa on the Pan Am flight to Honolulu. Under his supervision, the FBI Laboratory Explosives Unit reconstructed two bombs. Officials took the first one to the FAA Technical Center in Atlantic City, New Jersey, where the device was put in a DC-10 fuselage, set up in the same way the bomb on the Pan Am plane was. "An anthropomorphic dummy placed in a window seat was thrown across two seats in the aisle in a manner similar to the way the Japanese youth was killed on the Pan Am 747," said Billy Vincent.

Kline's hunch was right. Investigators concluded that the person or persons who had made the Rio bomb also had made the Honolulu bomb.

At the same time, the U.S. government stumbled onto a most fortuitous discovery. The bomb that Adnan had turned over in Geneva was being made available by the Swiss federal police. An analysis of that bomb showed that the explosive was 80 percent PETN and 20 percent rubber adhesive binder, covered with a cheesecloth material. There was also a subminiature audio jack, an E-Cell time-delay circuit, an electric detonator, and two AAA-size 1.5-volt batteries. "The wires were the same color and the components were assembled in the same way," recalled Kline.

In other words, there was one person responsible for assembling all three bombs.

7

Life in Switzerland

Adnan was given a Swiss passport and a new identity. He became Mario Rosatti. He wasn't asked too many prying questions but every once in a while someone would be confused by his supposed Italian heritage. Why then did he not speak or look Italian?

It was obviously not the best cover for him, but the Swiss asked him to take it. Maybe they had their own reasons.

Adnan would weave an intricate web of lies. His paternal grandfather was mostly Arab but partially Italian—thus explaining the surname—but his grandmother was entirely Lebanese. His father, actually three quarters Arab, married a Lebanese, and Mario was born in his mother's homeland.

It was a mind-boggler that even Adnan had a hard time keeping straight. Most inquisitive people were so befuddled by his genealogy that they didn't think to ask how and when he'd become a Swiss citizen. It was all too confusing.

Walking through the streets of Bern or late at night in

his apartment, Adnan thought about his real identity, his family, and his girlfriend. The Swiss intelligence passed along a few messages to Ronac for him but they had never again spoken since his defection. His family knew nothing of what had become of him; the worst part was knowing he'd never be able to tell them—it would put himself and them in too much danger.

The only consolation was that the people of Switzerland were very considerate and welcomed this newcomer who barely spoke of his past.

"I knew I had to start a new life in a new country with strange people, but they treated me well," Adnan said.

He began to make friends. One of his first acquaintances was a twenty-five-year-old blond, blue-eyed young woman from America named Christine. She said she lived in Utah. After meeting Adnan and briefly speaking to him, she asked if she could drop by his place later that night.

Adnan was beside himself. A beautiful woman had just invited herself over to see him. He bought flowers. And waited for her arrival.

She came equipped with the Bible and a friend who was also on a mission for the Mormon Church. This was a bit of a letdown, but Adnan still was intrigued. He smoked one cigarette after another, inviting them to join him. They told him it was against their religion. He offered them coffee. That too was against the rules.

At another time in his life Adnan might not have wasted his time listening to the teachings of another religion. He had his own. He was a Muslim. But his new existence, while free of terrorists, was lonely. At the time, becoming a Mormon sounded like a good idea. He started attending prayer meetings and was introduced to interesting people. He thought about moving to Utah.

When he wasn't studying the Scriptures he was still assisting the Swiss. He and Max would go to cafés and speak Arabic, hoping to overhear bits and pieces of conversations that might lead to the uncovering of terrorists.

At one point, shortly after Adnan had defected, Swiss intelligence asked Adnan if he would call Ibrahim. They wanted to put a tracer on the phone as well as tape-record the conversation. More than that, the Swiss had an idea—it was a long shot—that they could entrap Ibrahim. Adnan had been in Switzerland a little more than a month—and his absence from Iraq had surely made Ibrahim very suspicious; he would know there hadn't been a bombing of the Noga Hilton. Yet Ibrahim could not know with any certainty precisely what had happened to Adnan. The odds were pretty good, Swiss intelligence calculated, that Ibrahim might let his guard down in a phone call from him.

The phone rang in Baghdad. A woman's voice—Adnan immediately recognized it as belonging to Ibrahim's wife—answered.

"Hello. Is Abu Ibrahim at home?" he asked.

"Sorry, he is not," she replied.

"Well, I'd like to leave a message for him," he said as Swiss intelligence listened in. "I was not able to find a hotel room at the Noga Hilton, so I had to go to a different one. I've run out of money. Please let me know who to go to."

The trap was set. All they could do was wait to see if Ibrahim would take the bait. Adnan told the Swiss that he was sure Ibrahim would dispatch an operative. He wanted to be there just in case a spy tried to verify that he was indeed still staying at the hotel.

"The Swiss were not selfish," Adnan said. "They put

my interest before their own. They didn't want to risk my being at the hotel because they thought someone might already be in Geneva looking for me."

Abu Safe arrived in Geneva a couple of days later at the hotel Adnan had mentioned to Ibrahim's wife. He went to the front desk and asked for Mohammed Jassin Khalaf, the name on the false passport that Adnan had been using. At that moment, the Swiss police surrounded and arrested him. In his wallet they found $1,500 in American currency, a picture of Adnan, and a note for him from Abu Ibrahim.

It said: "My brother, please give your luggage to this man. He'll finish the mission. You are to return home at once."

When questioned why Abu Safe would want Adnan's luggage, he would say only that he was told he was to pick up drugs. The Swiss police suspected that his real mission had been to kill Adnan.

Safe was arrested and put in jail. The Swiss arranged for Adnan to be placed in the cell next to his. At the very least, Safe could report back to Ibrahim that Adnan had been arrested as well. The Swiss had placed a hidden microphone in the cell and Adnan was trying to coax Safe into talking. But every time he approached him, the man put his fingers over his mouth. Abu Safe wouldn't talk. It was obvious to Adnan that Abu Safe suspected Adnan of having collaborated with the Swiss.

The Swiss didn't know what to do with Abu Safe. He had done nothing illegal, yet it was clear he was a terrorist operative for Abu Ibrahim. They could easily have forced him to reveal everything he knew. They could even have made him "disappear." But Swiss counterterrorist officials were too genteel, too polite to deal effectively with terrorists.

Within two weeks, Safe was expelled from Switzerland. Though Safe requested to be sent back to Fatima, Adnan suggested they send him to Jordan instead. Jordan had a reputation for being severe with terrorists. Swiss intelligence reported that a month later Safe had been arrested by the Jordanians.

Starting in late August 1982 Adnan worked with Swiss authorities on several sting operations against suspected terrorists and false double agents.

Besides taking note of his security suggestions, the Swiss involved Adnan in their intelligence investigations. He was happy to oblige. He'd never been an idle person and his role as their assistant gave him a purpose in a new home where he neither spoke nor wrote the language. Other employment would have been close to impossible to come by.

The advantages for the Swiss were numerous. Adnan was one of the first Arab terrorists ever to turn himself over to a Western government and there was much to learn from him. Just as he had shown the West how the "invisible bombs" were defying all security systems, he could set them straight on more obvious cases too.

This became evident when the Swiss granted a Syrian Kurd named Hamza political asylum. According to Hamza, he was in grave danger—facing a court-ordered death sentence—for his political activism in Syria.

Adnan was immediately skeptical. Anyone from an Arab country would know that courts there are not democratic enough to go through the bureaucratic logistics of imposing a death sentence on political dissidents. Adnan laughed to himself. The West always seemed to forget that Arab countries were ruled by military dictators who didn't give a damn about human rights and even less of a damn about legal processes. They'd simply interrogate the accused, then execute. Hamza's account was hardly believable.

Adnan knew this would be an easy case to crack. His interpreter, Max, gave him the name of the restaurant where Hamza had reportedly been spending his time, and he began going there. Soon, because of their common Arab bond, Hamza and Adnan met. Adnan cultivated the friendship, hoping to extract information.

It didn't take long. After only a few weeks, Hamza confessed to Adnan that he had been operating under a false identity. His name was really Samir.

His story unraveled in a predictable way. Fleeing his past, he'd been on the fringes of terrorism as a bodyguard for Abu Jihad, the senior PLO commander and top aide to Yasser Arafat. Jihad was responsible for many bloody terrorist attacks on Israel. Years later, in 1988, Israeli commandos would kill him in an operation in Tunis.

Samir had initially revered his leader. When he was with Jihad in Arab countries, Jihad strictly followed the decorum, abiding by the rules a dedicated revolutionary would obey: He didn't drink, appeared to be devoted to his family, and led a simple life.

But soon Samir found that Jihad had two personalities. Much like Dr. Jekyll and Mr. Hyde, neither one bore any resemblance to the other. While traveling abroad with him, Samir witnessed Jihad drinking, having sex with teenage boys, and extravagantly tossing away money on frivolous whims.

As Samir began to trust Adnan, he offered to show him

some pictures of times past. "There's Jihad with the handsome boys in Bucharest," and "Here I am with Jihad," he said. Then Samir pulled out some other pictures. They weren't family albums. They were "casing" photographs of people Jihad intended to eliminate.

Adnan finally had proof. The next day he told Max about all of Samir's mementos and they devised a scheme to obtain them. By convincing Samir to let him borrow his room for part of an afternoon to seduce a woman, Adnan would have access.

The approach was perfect. Samir was very gracious and told Adnan to have a ball as he tossed the keys to him. Adnan found the incriminating evidence, quickly drove to the Swiss federal police headquarters, copied them, then returned them to Samir's apartment. The whole project took less than an hour.

The Swiss could no longer hesitate. They'd had their doubts before; now they had evidence. Soon after, Samir was deported to Germany.

While Adnan was content with having completed a successful mission, the experience was also painful. Samir had trusted him, revealed his true identity, and—without ever knowing it—had been in a similar situation as Adnan. Both had ideals once and were disillusioned with their country's leaders. The difference was that Samir at least took the chance to open up and confide in someone else. Adnan never felt secure enough to take that risk. He was dying just for the simple pleasure of telling someone his real name.

Meanwhile, the Americans had requested to speak with Adnan. "The Swiss were always democratic," he said. "They told me that if I didn't want to talk to them I didn't have to. It was up to me."

Adnan wanted to help.

This time it was higher-ups in the CIA, along with a couple of other officials. They had material that came from an explosion over Hawaii and asked if Adnan recognized its construction.

"I did," Adnan said. "It was Abu's invisible bomb."

The Americans were ecstatic and asked if Adnan would be available to come to the United States to serve as a witness against Mohammed Rashid.

"We'd like you to help us prosecute him," they said.

Adnan agreed.

By December 1983, the cold weather in Switzerland was beginning to bother Adnan. He'd already spent one winter there and found it terribly unpleasant. He asked the Swiss if he could go elsewhere. They said yes and thought that they could arrange to send him to Morocco. The first order of business was getting him a passport that wouldn't conflict so much with his background. The Swiss passport with the Italian name was good enough for inside Switzerland but it would never work abroad.

They spoke with the Lebanese government and were given a passport for Adnan. Now he became Mahmod al-Altie. The Swiss gave him the name of a French company in Morocco where he could work as an engineer and earn $60,000 a year.

Adnan spent seven months there. He loved the weather, had a splendid time fishing, and didn't work one solitary day. The French company he'd been referred to went bankrupt just after he arrived and he wasn't able to find other work. Adnan bought a Fiat, and spent every last cent the Swiss had provided him with to start a new life. He told them what happened and they suggested he come back to Switzerland at the end of August 1984. He moved to a suburb fifteen minutes outside of Bern, but lasted there only a month before he began longing for Morocco again.

His request to return was approved, but he had been back in Morocco only a few weeks when he received an urgent phone call. The Swiss asked him to return immediately.

He arrived in Switzerland on November 13, 1984, and went to the Swiss federal police. They told him that American officials were waiting for him. "They want to take you to America," they said, assuring him that if he'd rather stay in Switzerland he was welcome.

Meanwhile the picture of America that his friend in the Damascus laundromat had painted was still vivid. In America anything would be possible.

He met with the Hawaii U.S. attorney Dan Bent, who said that the United States would pursue Rashid, arrest him, and then prosecute. Adnan's role would be to testify against him. Bent said the process would take less than two years.

"How long will it take you to be ready?" Bent asked.

"I'm ready right now," Adnan said.

On November 17, they left for America.

"I wore a gray suit with a heavy overcoat," Adnan said. "It was so cold."

The group of Americans who accompanied him included Dan Bent, a woman from the Justice Department, and two federal marshals who were over six feet tall. Adnan stared at their shoes.

"I'd never seen shoes so big," he said.

They went to the airport and Adnan could tell they were carrying guns. The officers also showed him their wallets with the star of the U.S. Marshals Service.

On the plane from Switzerland to New York, Bent and Adnan tried to communicate but it was difficult. "We were mostly using sign language," Adnan said.

They switched planes in New York and went on to Washington, D.C. As he walked out of the terminal, getting his first glimpse of America, Adnan was stunned.

"I saw all of my dream cars," he said. "Limousines, big Cadillacs. It was just as I'd imagined—but this was for *real.*"

Security was everywhere. He was ushered into a car with dark windows. At first he didn't realize that it was sandwiched between two others. "But when you see three cars always going in the same direction you catch on," he said.

Adnan was taken to a hotel in downtown Washington, where he was placed in one suite and the security people, with their walkie-talkies, were right next door in another. Even the waitress bringing room service had to be identified.

"All the security made me much more nervous than I had been in a long time," Adnan said. "I began thinking, 'Maybe they know something that I don't.'"

The next day, after a complete medical exam, Adnan met with Stanley Morris, head of the U.S. Marshals Service. On the way to his office, Adnan passed lots of flags, and pictures with noble-looking people holding guns. The chief marshal had an expansive office. "He was a big strong man," Adnan said, "who I imagined living in Texas."

Morris said that Adnan would become a member of the Federal Witness Protection Program. "You'll be under my care," he said. Adnan thought it all seemed so efficient, reliable, and reassuring. Ibrahim would be no match for the United States.

President Reagan's Arabic translator was also at the meeting. He said Adnan was welcome in the United States and asked where he wanted to live.

"I told him I hated the cold," Adnan said.

They tossed around a few ideas. Adnan was keen on Hollywood, remembering the Jerry Lewis and Dean Martin films from his days in Damascus. The palm trees, the convertible . . . it all would be perfect. The marshals suggested he choose something that would be convenient to Washington—since he would be traveling a lot during the trial. They settled on Miami.

"I am going to live in the best country in the world," Adnan thought to himself. "America is democracy. America is a superpower. America is freedom."

8

Getting off the List

For America's counterterrorism officials, Adnan's arrival on their turf was big news, providing a cornerstone in the growing body of evidence against Saddam Hussein's logistical and financial support for terrorist organizations.

Now if only the United States would use it.

Information on Saddam's terror ties had come from other sources besides Adnan, but mainly the kinds of substandard sources intelligence services must make do with: scraps of electronically intercepted information and unconfirmed reports from unreliable people. Adnan was a living and breathing witness, an eyewitness to one of the most closed societies in the world. He'd been vetted by all the appropriate authorities and had a universally understandable motive for talking: He was scared, scared out of his wits.

With the totality of the other evidence on Saddam Hussein's terrorist connections, Adnan's story brought the case against the Iraqi leader to a critical mass.

"Iraq was one of the prime sponsors of terrorism throughout the world; the evidence wasn't even subject to question or interpretation," recalled Howard Teicher, former National Security Council director for the Middle East and senior director for Political-Military Affairs. Teicher had been appointed to the National Security Council in 1982 and was responsible for, among other things, collecting information and helping to set policy on counterterrorism. In the Reagan administration, he had been involved in the most senior policy discussions of all Middle East matters. "Iraq was a country on which we routinely received intelligence reports—that it was facilitating acts of terror against Israeli and American targets."

Iraq's Mukhabarat was one of the most savage intelligence agencies in the world. It governed the country with a barbaric hand, killing political dissidents at will. Those who were suspected of possible espionage against Iraq were dealt with by the Mukhabarat in a special way. Fingers were cut off in interrogation sessions, electrodes attached to genitals, eyeballs split open with razors. Then, death. It was no wonder that Iranian and Syrian spies often killed themselves if they saw that arrest was imminent.

The Mukhabarat was headed by Saddam Hussein's half brother and cousin, Barzan al-Tikriti, who took over the organization in 1974. Tikriti, who became perhaps Saddam Hussein's closest associate, maintained a close relationship with Iraq's military intelligence, another brutal arm of the Iraqi government. Essentially, Tikriti had control over both organizations, giving him extraordinary power, not just at home but around the world. U.S. intelligence had obtained indisputable hard evidence that Tikriti was in communication with Iraqi embassies and routinely ordered the transfer of explosives and weapons for terrorist attacks around the globe.

Adnan could shed some light on this network, but there was plenty of other evidence on it available to the CIA and other Western intelligence agencies. Tikriti, according to agency officials, was also operationally responsible for orchestrating terror attacks through surrogate Palestinian groups located all over the world. In 1983, Tikriti would leave his post as head of the Mukhabarat and become Iraq's representative to the United Nations in Geneva. From there, he would continue to plot terrorist attacks—in fact, the Iraqi embassy in Switzerland, according to American and Israeli intelligence sources, would in short time become the nerve center for much Iraqi-supported terrorism in Europe.

For intelligence analysts, agents, and counterterrorist officials, whose job it was to stop terrorism, the fact that Iraq had been included on the list of countries supporting international terrorism was very important. The list was established by Congress in 1979 under the Export Administration Act. It required the State Department to issue a list once a year, based on intelligence reports, that declared which countries supported international terrorism. Being on the list was not just a moral stigma; a country deemed supportive of international terrorism was denied American military sales or any sensitive technology. For the intelligence community, there was an added, though unofficial, reason that being listed was so serious: It allowed the CIA, Defense Intelligence Agency, National Security Council, and the Justice Department to focus efforts on monitoring, tracking, and preventing acts of terrorism that originated within the listed country. In other words, being on the terrorism list meant giving the United States a mandate to contain the country—and expend whatever resources were needed, which could include recruiting agents or setting up listening posts.

The corollary was also true: If a country was *not* on the list, the bureaucratic justification for expending money and agents on getting good intelligence on it could be seriously weakened. So U.S. counterterrorism officials considered the list an important tool. From 1979 on, they had used it not just against Iraq but against Syria, North Korea, South Yemen, and Libya.

Then, suddenly, after three years, this tool was no longer usable against Iraq. The news came as a rude awakening to counterterrorist officials in February 1982. Incredibly, despite the evidence collected by the CIA and the Pentagon, the State Department found that Iraq no longer provided support or sanctuary for terrorists. Noel Koch, as director of special planning at the Pentagon from 1981 through 1984, was responsible for the Pentagon's counterterrorist operations and units. The outspoken Koch participated in the interagency group that met frequently to coordinate the administration's response to terrorist threats and share intelligence. Known as the Terrorist Incident Working Group, these officials, who included representatives from the CIA, FBI, and National Security Council, discussed Iraqi support for terrorism in great detail. The fact that Iraq was about to be taken off the list came as an unpleasant surprise.

Koch felt that Iraq "deserved to be on that list. I called my State Department colleagues, my counterparts at the Office for Combatting Terrorism, and I asked them why Iraq was being taken off. It was pretty clear to me that this was a decision made at higher levels—and that it was made irrespective of Iraq's role in terrorism. They felt there were other reasons to cultivate a better relationship with Iraq. And that obviously had to do with the Iran-Iraq war. It was our policy to tilt against Iran and therefore anybody that was against Iran deserved our support. We didn't agree with that. We thought that Iraq was a dangerous country then and would *continue* to be a dangerous country."

But other voices in the Reagan administration carried the day, particularly through the policy's influential proponents at the State Department's Bureau of Near Eastern and South Asian Affairs. The reason: Iraq's increasingly bloody war against Iran, America's nemesis-of-the-moment in the Persian Gulf. The policy had been prompted by the fear that Iran could militarily defeat Iraq in the Iran-Iraq war, which had started in 1980 when Saddam Hussein attacked Iraq. Saddam's vision of quick victory, spurred by his capture of the Shatt-al-Arab waterway, soon vanished. The Iranians began to fight harder than anyone expected. By late 1981, Iran had scored several strategic victories against Iraq and was on the verge of cutting off Iraq's only access to the sea, the port city of Basra. American policy swung into action to stop an Iranian victory.

Richard Murphy was assistant secretary of state for Near Eastern affairs from October 1983 through 1989. Though he was not head of the NEA Department at the time of the policy shift, he recalled the rationale: "If there was any consideration that guided the decision of the [Reagan] administration not to put Iraq on the states-supporting-terrorism list, it was the very hostile atmosphere towards Iran in those days, a result going back to the occupation of the embassy in 1979 and very deep worry about Iranian fundamentalist Islam, the activities they were funding in Lebanon, and the threat that we saw to our many friends in the area from Iran."

The State Department wasn't the only major supporter of the policy change. At the National Security Council, there were fierce debates, but the pro-Iraqi faction won. Top National Security Council aide Don Fortier and his colleague Howard Teicher were both shot down when they pushed for the United States to slow down this complete reversal in policy. At the CIA, director William Casey became a strong advocate of a tilt toward Iraq, so much so that, according to former intelligence and Reagan administration officials, he actually traveled to Baghdad in early 1982 to meet with Saddam Hussein. That the head of the CIA would secretly travel to and meet with the head of a state that regularly used terrorism as an instrument of foreign policy had shocked the few people who knew about the trip. The extraordinary and unreported meeting set in motion a clandestine intelligence relationship between the United States and Iraq that would last for the next six years. But it would be a one-way relationship; the United States would provide satellite and aerial reconnaissance photos of the Iranian troop formations to the Iraqis. The Iraqis, in turn, would use the information to counter what would otherwise have been successful Iranian offensives. According to Reagan administration officials, Lt. Col. Oliver North had insisted that Saddam would provide information on terrorist groups to the United States in exchange for that military intelligence. But officials who have studied the intelligence "take" from the tilt-toward-Baghdad years say the information provided by Saddam Hussein was "pure disinformation" and "worse than totally worthless."

In any event, shortly after Casey returned from his meeting with Saddam, President Reagan signed a classified national security directive mandating the change in U.S. policy toward Iraq.

On February 26, 1982, the State Department officially removed Iraq from the list of countries supporting international terrorism. As if it knew the embarrassment that would ensue, State made no public announcement of the change. The policy reversal was simply listed in the *Federal Register,* a daily tome published by the federal government to formally enumerate the thousands of changes in U.S. regulations and laws.

The terse announcement in the *Federal Register* was spelled out in fewer than three sentences. But what it really spelled was one of the most shortsighted and dangerously counterproductive shifts in American policy undertaken in the 1980s: The door was opened for "normalization" of relations with Iraq. That effectively translated into a rush to export billions of dollars of sensitive technology, computers, trucks, helicopters, agricultural commodities. The "normalization" spawned a wide net of powerful vested economic interests with Baghdad and with that, powerful supporters and lobbyists who would make sure that it became impossible to reverse policy toward Iraq—no matter what intelligence reports said about the country's politics and embrace of terrorist acts. By the end of 1982, the United States would be supplying top-secret intelligence to Iraq.

Here was a change of enormous significance, yet five months earlier, the CIA had been apprised of Adnan's defection to Switzerland. A universally credited witness—with direct and firsthand knowledge of an Iraqi-backed terrorist group that had mounted a multicontinent aircraft bombing campaign just months before—was still living in

Switzerland. Why couldn't those who knew about him get his story out?

During the next few years, officials like Vince Cannistraro at the CIA and Noel Koch at the Pentagon tried to make the case that Saddam Hussein was operating the functional equivalent of Murder Incorporated. They argued at policy meetings, at the interagency counterterrorist meetings, that Iraq had continued to back terrorism and used its diplomatic facilities to transfer weapons and provide cover for terrorists. At the FBI, there was deep anger at the policy taken by the government. "We knew that Iraq was working hand in hand with Abu Ibrahim and several other terrorist groups," recalled FBI explosives expert Denny Kline, "and we tried to argue that we had do something to block the madman from continuing to carry out bomb attacks against the United States."

At the middle level of senior Washington officialdom, those handling the intelligence and working with the victims of terrorism were acutely aware of the degree to which Saddam Hussein had created a secret branch of terrorists that carried out his "hits" while at the same time giving him plausible deniability. There were heated arguments at the National Security Council, at the CIA, at the Office for Combatting Terrorism in the State Department, and at the Pentagon.

But it was to no avail. Casey had Reagan's ear and Iran was considered too great a foe—too many people in high places in Washington were willing to look the other way when it came to Saddam's support for terrorists like Abu Ibrahim. Saddam Hussein decided to take advantage of America's new policy shift.

In April 1982, barely a month after Iraq had been removed from the terrorism list, the Iraqi president decided to respond to the American move toward appeasement. It was a response that he would employ repeatedly over the next nine years—a response that would take immediate advantage of his newfound respectability.

According to intelligence intercepts of Iraqi communications between Baghdad and selected embassies in Europe and Asia, Baghdad instructed its Mukhabarat intelligence officers around the world to shop around for a major terrorist target to attack that could somehow provoke Israel into retaliating against the heavily armed forces of the Palestine Liberation Organization in Lebanon. Intelligence analysts later concluded that Saddam wanted to draw Israel into a war in Lebanon, which could then provide a diplomatic fig leaf Saddam could use as a pretext to declare a truce in his losing battle with Teheran and claim they both needed to fight the larger "Zionist enemy."

According to the intelligence agencies that monitored the communications, the Iraqi embassy in London responded to the call. It reported back to Baghdad that it had under surveillance Israeli and Jewish targets whose security could be easily breached. One of these was the Israeli ambassador, Shlomo Argov.

In the meantime, the Iraqi government had hedged its bets by assigning one its chief resident terrorists, Abu Nidal, the role of carrying out the attack in London. Nidal, who had mounted some of the most vicious terror attacks in the world against Israeli, American, and Jewish civilians, already had an infrastructure in place.

Abu Nidal is the *nom de guerre* (it means "Father of Struggle") for a Palestinian whose real name is Sabri Khalil al-Banna. He was born in 1936 in Palestine in the city of Jaffa, outside Tel Aviv. Though he had collaborated with PLO leader Yasser Arafat in the 1960s, Nidal split with Arafat over the PLO's decision in 1974 to accept the idea of the existence of Israel. Arafat decided to focus his terrorist operations "only" against Israel on Israeli soil and the occupied territories. That was too much for Nidal, and he moved to Baghdad, where he set up his renegade Fatah Revolutionary Council. Its avowed aim: to kill Israelis, Jews, and Americans. Nidal also directed his deadly rage at moderate Palestinians, threatening to kill Yasser Arafat. Nidal was believed to be behind the periodic killing of moderate Palestinians in Europe and the West Bank.

Nidal entrusted his operation in Great Britain to a top operative, Nawaf Rosan, a Palestinian who had been living in London since the fall of 1981 as a "student" learning English. The thirty-six-year-old was more than just an operative for Nidal; he had become an officer in the Iraqi Mukhabarat shortly after he had moved to Baghdad in 1981. Rosan recruited three other accomplices, but carefully made sure that they were unaware of those who were providing the weapons and support for the operation. Together, Rosan and his confederates collected intelligence on the whereabouts of Ambassador Argov as well as two prominent British Jews. Weapons were distributed to the Abu Nidal cell from the Iraqi embassy in London. These weapons, British and American intelligence officials later discovered, had been transported to the embassy through Iraq's diplomatic pouch.

On the evening of June 3, 1982, the Israeli ambassador attended a reception given by the De La Rue textile company at the Dorchester Hotel. In attendance were more than one hundred ambassadors and foreign diplomatic officials. At about 11 P.M., Argov left the reception and walked toward his diplomatic car parked outside the hotel's entrance on Park Lane. Suddenly, a man dressed in a sleeveless shirt walked up behind Argov. It was Rosan's accomplice. He pulled out an automatic pistol, and shot him at point-blank range in the head. Argov fell to the ground with bullet wounds to his brain. An armed policeman shot and wounded the assailant in the course of a brief, unsuccessful chase. Several hours later, Rosan was picked up by police. A trial the following year resulted in Rosan's conviction and he was sentenced to thirty-five years in jail. Miraculously, Ambassador Argov survived the attack, but he was left totally paralyzed.

Following the attempted assassination, State Department officials recalled, the United States privately "protested" to Iraq that Abu Nidal, who publicly claimed credit for it, had continued to receive "refuge" in Baghdad. "Refuge" implied that Iraq was barely tolerating Nidal. In fact, the Iraqi Mukhabarat continued, in 1982 and in the first half of 1983, to provide intelligence and weapons to Nidal's training camps in Iraq. But Nidal didn't just depend on government handouts; he also ran several "legitimate" businesses in Iraq. One such enterprise was a chicken farm outside of Baghdad, which apparently generated hefty sums for his organization.

Even the State Department could not ignore the intelligence reports. American embassy officials continued to hold talks with the Iraqi foreign ministry, where the subject of Abu Nidal was repeatedly brought up. Finally, in mid-1983, under American pressure, Abu Nidal left Baghdad, relocating his headquarters in Damascus. The following spring, again as a response to American pressure, Iraq "closed down" Abu Nidal's public relations office in Baghdad. The State Department portrayed this as a victory—and the result of heavy and successful diplomatic pressure. But at the CIA, reports of clandestine Iraqi ties to Nidal continued to be collected around the world.

With Abu Nidal getting "booted" out of Baghdad, the State Department insisted that its policy of weaning Iraq away from terrorism was working. Recalled Assistant Secretary of State Richard Murphy, "We didn't turn a blind eye toward Iraqi terrorism but we felt the trend against terrorism was working. It was having some success."

Whether it was out of hopeless naïveté or simple myopia, the State Department could not even fathom the idea that perhaps Iraqi officials were lying to the United States when they denied they were supporting terrorism. Once again, State seemed so willing to indulge in wishful thinking—as long as Iraq was at war with Iran—that those officials who knew about Adnan were completely stymied in getting his story out or even getting him to the United States. Murphy was the point man at the State Department who dealt with the Iraqi foreign minister and the Iraqi embassy in Washington. "The people I was dealing with—the foreign minister and the [Iraqi] ambassador—I don't see how they [could have] thought they were able to cover stuff up. They knew the extent of our intelligence effort against terrorism and how seriously the president and secretary of state took terrorism and had made it a major issue in their administration. I don't think they would have been stupid enough to lie to us, so I assume they were telling the truth—that the [terrorist] operation had been closed down at some point in early 1984." But in fact, according to American, Israeli, and British intelligence officials, Iraq continued to orchestrate terror attacks.

Iraq was able to do this through Abu Ibrahim, who stayed in Baghdad and went about his business—the business of planning major terrorist attacks on American and Israeli targets. What the American pressure on Baghdad succeeded in doing was focus Ibrahim's attacks exclusively on Israeli or Jewish targets in Europe, such as El Al flights or synagogues. By not striking explicitly at American airplanes, Abu Ibrahim, in a bizarre way, met the State Department requirements that he cease his role in terrorism.

Throughout the early-to-mid-1980s, the State Department persisted in believing—or at least professing to believe—that the Iraqi-based terrorists were, as Baghdad had insisted, "retired." The only one who had physically left Iraq was Abu Nidal—but even he, according to U.S. intelligence, continued to maintain surreptitious ties to Iraqi intelligence officers.

What the State Department's Bureau of Near Eastern and South Asian Affairs and others in the Reagan administration had done was selectively remove Saddam Hussein's support for Palestinian terrorist groups as part of the yardstick that had been used to measure state-supported terrorism. By being officially blind to the Iraqi-supported or engineered Palestinian terrorist attacks on Israeli targets, the United States had effectively given Saddam Hussein the green light to continue his support for terrorism.

At the State Department, there was disagreement with the "official" line that Iraq had ceased to support terrorism, even among those sympathetic to the policy shift. Terry Arnold was deputy director of the State Department's Office for Combatting Terrorism until 1984. That office was responsible for collecting information on international terrorism and making sure it was factored into U.S. policy. Arnold recalled the dilemma: "There were several Palestinian groups there at the time Iraq was removed from the list. . . . And it was a situation in which those groups were present and continued to be present. But the issue for the State Department and for the executive branch was what were the chances of influencing Saddam Hussein away from his support for terrorism."

Arnold continued, "Can we do that best by leaving him off the list and working with him or can we reach him by the sanctions of putting him on the list? This was the basic debate. I don't honestly believe that debate was about whether or not Saddam Hussein continued to give certain sanctuary to terrorist groups. He did and everyone knew that. . . . Through this period, it's fair to say that Saddam Hussein continued to lend sanctuary and a degree of support to elements of the Palestinian movement."

Because the evidence of Saddam Hussein's support for Palestinian terrorism was so overwhelmingly persuasive, it became necessary to concoct a cover story for public consumption. Recalled State Department official Murphy, "We were told that these men were out of business, that they had been veterans of earlier activities on behalf of Palestinian terrorist elements, but that they had been retired." It was the type of explanation that Mafia members had disseminated when they wanted to take the heat off—they would say they had "retired" and were no longer in "business." Police and federal prosecutors always knew that one never retired from the mob—and that these declarations of "retirement" were totally disingenuous. Similarly, intelligence analysts at the CIA knew that there was no truth to the Iraqi declarations. But at the State Department, Iraq's explanations were blindly accepted, for one simple and important reason: The State Department could not afford to undermine its new policy of tilting toward Iraq. If the terrorists weren't really "retired," then Iraq would have to be put back on the list of countries supporting terrorism.

But not everyone in the Reagan administration was buying the Iraqi explanation. Various officials, such as the National Security Council's Howard Teicher, the CIA's Vince Cannistraro, and the Pentagon's Noel Koch, rejected State's views.

Koch vividly remembered the fiction being perpetuated at Foggy Bottom. "This was a very poetic arrangement. It involved the willing suspension of disbelief on the part of the American diplomatic community. And so, if we chose not to believe that Iraq was involved in terrorism, we didn't."

It was a fiction that had to be constantly reinforced, particularly at State, which was vulnerable to the charge that it was cooking the raw intelligence information. Assistant Secretary of State Murphy, one of the chief proponents of the new policy toward Iraq, actually became convinced that Abu Ibrahim no longer was active as of 1984. "I recall that we had discussions with the Iraqi authorities—the specific dates I cannot tell you offhand, but [in] 1984 and 1985 [we were] assured that while the evidence was that he remained in Baghdad, he was out of business and they would ensure that he stayed out of business."

Asked whether it was possible, in retrospect, that Iraq had lied to the United States, Murphy said, "At that point in time I don't think they would have any reason to lie to us. They were interested in getting what support they could for Iraq's position vis-à-vis Iran in the war, but they had reason to believe we would check out reports and continue to be vigilant to any evidence of terrorism activity organized in Baghdad and that we would come after them if there were any such."

In fact, the United States never officially issued any warnings. Not surprisingly, Iraqi found that it could literally get away with murder—and it continued to support and fund repeated acts of terrorism.

If only Murphy and his co-believers had been able or willing to read of Adnan's firsthand account of his meetings with Ibrahim, it might have had a profound effect on their thinking, as it would have had on other senior policymakers responsible for maintaining the tilt toward Baghdad.

But alas, it was not to be.

9

The Hunt for Rashid

Adnan's handlers, those most anxious to have him tell what he knew about Saddam Hussein's terror network, had a lot of work to do. At the FBI, the news that Iraq was out of the terror game and that Abu Ibrahim had "retired" came as a shock to Denny Kline. The FBI's chief bomb sleuth continued to be on the other end of Ibrahim's receiving line: His bombs were turning up all over the world—in Rome, Brussels, Sydney, Lisbon, and Paris. Several had been found after they malfunctioned; most, however, had been intercepted by intelligence agencies before they could be planted. At that point either Kline would be sent to examine the bombs or the bombs would be sent to the United States.

Looking for the bombs' "signatures" was tedious work. The endless hours spent sitting in a laboratory was quite a change of pace for Kline, who had been a star athlete in college, first at Vanderbilt, which he attended on a football scholarship, then as a transfer student at Georgia Southern, where he was a baseball player. Afterward he stayed in Georgia and became a high school football coach. His first team had a record of 7-3. After several years, he made the dramatic switch of becoming an FBI agent.

On the surface, it seemed as if there could not be two fields more professionally different than football coach and FBI agent. But when Kline joined the FBI, he recalled, he went from "developing characters to catching characters."

The common denominator was that both professions revolved around problem solving. Just as he had devised his own strategy for winning football games, Kline was the chief tactician behind the FBI cases on which he worked. When he was on his counterterrorism cases, he was his own boss—and would rise or fall upon the success of his own strategy. When an arrest would finally be made, it was like Friday night at the football stadium: His adrenaline would flow; the excitement and satisfaction would hit hard when all the work he'd put into the case finally came together.

For Kline, the only thing missing from the Abu Ibrahim case was Friday night. He had conclusively identified as many as fifteen bombs made by Ibrahim, yet the master bomb maker was not even close to being caught. He was worried that the satisfaction of completing the game against Abu Ibrahim would ultimately elude him.

Throughout Washington, Ibrahim was becoming far too familiar to the core of officials who worked counterterrorism for the Reagan administration. He was a "household name" among those whose mission in life was to track terrorists or their paths of destruction. At the Pentagon, Noel Koch would routinely see intelligence reports citing Ibrahim's activities. At the FAA, Billy Vincent would get reports from foreign aviation and intelligence officials of

Ibrahim's attempts to bomb airplanes. At the National Security Council, Howard Teicher would sit in on meetings and get detailed briefings on Iraq's strong terrorist hand—and Abu Ibrahim's name was always the one most mentioned.

Across the Potomac River, Ibrahim's name kept popping up in the CIA's intelligence traffic. "Abu Ibrahim was up to his eyeballs in terrorism—and he was being financed and supported by the Mukhabarat," recalled a CIA operations officer. The CIA made an active decision to track Ibrahim and members of his organization.

But unfortunately for the CIA, Ibrahim rarely moved from his well-guarded headquarters in downtown Baghdad. He had openly talked about his fears of being assassinated or abducted by the CIA or the Mossad. His fears were probably justified, but there was no way anyone could get at him, unless an operation was run in Baghdad—which was considered too dangerous, both physically and politically.

Fortunately for the intelligence community, however, Ibrahim's key operative evinced no such fears of traveling and moving about. Mohammed Rashid traveled all around the world, where he would recruit new couriers, rent safe houses, and conduct casings of likely bomb targets. The CIA had managed to obtain copies of the three false passports that Rashid would routinely use when traveling abroad. And with that information, the CIA was able to track him.

This tracking was not done on a real-time basis. Rather, when Rashid went through the passport control of a foreign country or made airline reservations, the CIA was notified. Sometimes the notification took hours; at other times the reports would be sent to CIA headquarters in

Langley days and weeks after Rashid was spotted. But the reports showed that Rashid was exceptionally active. He would frequently travel to Bangkok, for example, renting houses in the middle of the city, and then conduct surveillance on Israeli commercial offices.

Rashid was tracked to Australia, where he made a failed attempt to bomb an Israeli office. He was also tracked to Singapore, Sweden, Germany, Athens, and Rome. Because he was so incredibly active, the CIA kicked up its counterterrorist investigation of him and his cohorts. With the help of other intelligence services, the CIA began to actively recruit informants in the May 15 Organization.

By 1984, the CIA was considering ways to "snatch" Rashid and bring him back to the United States to stand trial. Though there had been some talk of simply doing away with him, thus avoiding the messy aspects of a trial and possible retaliation by Ibrahim, it was quickly and roundly dismissed: If terrorists were to be taught a lesson, they would have to be tried under the rules of the game the West set—that is, under the rule of law.

To catch Rashid, it would be necessary to lie in wait for him. He was certainly not the first terrorist who would be the planned target of an abduction in the Reagan administration. The idea had begun to gain credence at the National Security Council under the guidance of Lt. Col. Oliver North. The Justice Department had ruled years back that kidnapping terrorists for trial in the United States was legally permissible.

One of the first objects of extensive abduction planning was Imad Mugniyah, the Lebanese terrorist who was— and still is—in charge of most of the American hostages still held in Lebanon, including Associated Press reporter Terry Anderson, who has been held the longest. North planned to have American agents kidnap Mugniyah on one of his secret trips to France. But the operation was scrubbed at the last minute when Mugniyah decided abruptly not to make the trip.

Before any abduction could even be planned, it was imperative to acquire as much as possible "real-time" intelligence on Ibrahim and Rashid. Certainly one of the ways to infiltrate Ibrahim's organization would have been to bring Adnan into the middle of things. He knew details about Ibrahim that no one else did. Shockingly, no one asked him anything. "In retrospect," recalled the FBI's Denny Kline, "the government should have been using Adnan Awad." One possibility would have been to have Adnan call Ibrahim or Rashid—even though they had long suspected that he had defected. Though it would obviously have been a long shot—after all, it had been tried once before by the Swiss—telephone calls by Adnan to other Ibrahim operatives might have produced traces of intelligence that would have proved instrumental to the CIA's surveillance. But Adnan continued to live sequestered in the United States, oblivious to what the CIA was trying to do.

Having failed to develop the necessary information on its own, the CIA turned to other Middle East intelligence services to see if they could help penetrate the May 15 Organization. Tunisian intelligence indicated they would be receptive. In previous years, the United States—and in particular the CIA—had developed extraordinarily good relations with key officials of Tunisia's intelligence service. Still, if there ever was any public disclosure, cooperating with the United States on a counterterrorist operation could be very embarrassing, particularly on an operation involving a prominent Palestinian like Abu Ibrahim. The Tunisians were themselves scared of being targeted by radical Palestinians, especially since the entire PLO enterprise was now on Tunisian soil. Despite these qualms, the Tunisian agency agreed to work with the CIA in trying to infiltrate Ibrahim's group.

One day, Tunisian officials told the CIA that one of Abu Ibrahim's couriers—who had been personally recruited by Rashid—had given himself up in Tunis before carrying out a bombing attack in Europe. Although he met with U.S. intelligence officials only once, he impressed them as being genuine. He spoke very little English. Tunisian officials told the Americans that he had agreed to become a double agent for Tunisia. The plan was to send him back to Baghdad, where he would volunteer to go on another mission for Abu Ibrahim. The CIA agreed to the plan.

But shortly after he left to go to Baghdad, something happened to the man, though just exactly what the CIA never found out. A month after he was dispatched to Baghdad via Amman, Jordan, he disappeared, never to be heard from again. To the CIA, this suggested several possible explanations: He was executed by Abu Ibrahim; the Tunisians decided to keep him as their exclusive agent; or the man simply ran away. Circumstantial evidence collected later suggested that the man was executed.

Even though the CIA had been able to monitor Rashid's travels, it was in the frustrating position of still not being able to stop him and other May 15 operatives from carrying out their attacks. One of those operatives was a Jordanian-born Palestinian named Fouad Hussein Shara.

Adnan knew many of Ibrahim's operatives, but Shara wasn't one of them. They had come from vastly different backgrounds. Perhaps it was a sign of the degree to which Ibrahim began diversifying his operations or the degree to which he had given day-to-day control over to Rashid.

Born in 1955 in East Jerusalem, Shara bounced around the Middle East and Europe after his adolescence. He was working in Italy for a car dealership when he was approached in early 1982 by an Ibrahim agent. The man invited Shara to come work in Baghdad for a Palestinian, but didn't tell him too much more than that. With a paid ticket in hand, the Ibrahim agent escorted Shara to Baghdad, where he met with Ibrahim. The chief terrorist told Shara that Israel needed to be attacked because it had stolen Palestinian land.

Shara was not heavily into politics, although, like many Palestinians, he hated Israel. He was more enticed by Abu Ibrahim's offer of a full-time job that paid well and involved sight-seeing excursions around the world. For the perennially insolvent Shara, the prospect of earning $1,000 a month was too good to pass up, particularly if it involved striking back at the Jews. Abu Ibrahim promised him a great future.

Shara lived in one of Ibrahim's multiple safe houses in Baghdad, traveling abroad on practice missions. Frequently, he would go to Thailand (which contained numerous Ibrahim and Nidal safe houses), Greece, England, and Italy to collect intelligence on possible targets. Jewish-owned stores and hotels were often cased, as were El Al offices.

In late 1982, Shara was readied for his first mission: bombing the American naval base near Naples. Traveling under a false passport provided by Mohammed Rashid,

Shara flew to Rome, where he picked up another Ibrahim agent. From there they drove to Naples, where the other agent tried to infiltrate a remote perimeter of the base. He couldn't gain access, so instead put a bomb in the garage of an American. The bomb failed to explode. Shara returned to Baghdad, where Abu Ibrahim dispatched him once again to the American base, but this time Shara was to plant the bomb personally. Ibrahim gave him a bomb that contained two pounds of Semtex. Shara traveled to Naples, where he placed the bomb near the American tennis club. Again, however, the bomb failed to explode.

Returning once more to Baghdad, Shara was confronted by an angry Abu Ibrahim, who apparently was very suspicous because there had been no explosion. Shara feared that the worst was in store for him. He got off lightly, though; he was not sent off on one of Ibrahim's notorious "one-way" missions. Instead, he was placed under "house arrest" in Baghdad and not allowed to leave for nine months.

By the fall of 1983, Shara had been "rehabilitated" and was given an opportunity to carry out part of a planned Ibrahim airplane terrorist spectacular. The weapon of choice was the barometric bomb. And thanks to Adnan and the suitcase bomb he had turned over to the authorities in Switzerland, law-enforcement and intelligence agencies around the globe had a precise fix on just how the master bomb maker confected his deadly devices. The assiduous work of people like Denny Kline at the FBI, and Billy Vincent and Walter Korsgaard at the Federal Aviation Administration, ensured that the United States knew exactly what to look for. But the bombs were still invisible.

Ibrahim had not been successful in bombing an airplane since the 1982 Honolulu attack. Now he was going to make sure that his bomb was smuggled on board without risk of disclosure by cleaning crews or airline security experts, who inspected the plane after each flight. A CIA report prepared in late 1983 uncannily forewarned what would happen. "There is a reasonable likelihood that Abu Ibrahim may try to attack an American or Israeli aircraft during the next five months."

Shara was told what he had to do. He went to Athens sometime in the fall of 1983 and stayed in one of the multiple apartments that Rashid and others had rented. He met up with an old friend with whom he'd worked in a factory some years before. This friend, in turn, introduced him to a British woman named Diane Coddling, whom Shara befriended. Shara offered Coddling an opportunity to make some money picking up some religious artifacts from a business colleague of Shara's in Israel. Shara told her she would fly to Tel Aviv on Olympic Airways, but on the return would have to fly from Tel Aviv to London, then London to Athens.

She would also have to take with her a special suitcase that could protect the religious artifacts from breakage. Coddling agreed and, in the process, unwittingly signed her own death warrant.

Shara flew back to Baghdad, where he picked up a suitcase from Ibrahim. Concealed in the lining were 350 grams of Semtex, neatly sewn into a one-by-eight-inch strip. The bomb was triggered by a barometric sensor hidden in the handle. The difference between this bomb and the other Abu Ibrahim bombs in the possession of the United States was, according to a report later compiled by Denny Kline, "the presence of a barometric pressure switch, which would cause the bomb to [detonate] as the plane was ascending during takeoff."

Shara returned to Athens with the suitcase and gave Coddling her airline tickets—but not the suitcase with the bomb. He gave her an empty suitcase. She was to have a trial run. Coddling flew to Tel Aviv and returned to Athens, as instructed. The ruse worked perfectly. Now it was time for the real thing.

In January 1984, Coddling left again for Tel Aviv. In Israel, she met with her contact, as previously arranged by Shara, who filled the suitcase with religious artifacts the day before she was scheduled to leave. He also triggered the timing device that would ignite the barometric fuse once it reached a certain altitude.

The next day, Coddling boarded her flight from Tel Aviv to London, taking with her the special suitcase. There were more than 260 other passengers on the jet. But though the plane stayed at a sufficiently high altitude for much of the four-hour trip, the bomb did not explode, apparently due to a malfunction in the timer. Coddling returned shortly to Athens, leaving the suitcase in London, where she had removed the contents she would be selling. When she contacted Shara to tell him she had returned, Shara asked her for the suitcase. She told him it was still in London, but agreed to go back there and retrieve it.

At the same time, airport officials in Istanbul had made a startling finding. A Palestinian had booked a flight to New York. The first leg of his trip was on Alitalia to Rome. In Rome, he was to transfer to a Pan Am flight to Kennedy Airport. Two hours before the flight's scheduled departure, the man checked his bag. But when boarding for the flight began, he failed to show up. Airport security officials ordered the bag removed from the plane. Demolitions experts opened it up—and found that it contained more than a pound of Semtex. It was wired with a barometric triggering mechanism and set to be triggered on the Rome–to–New York leg of the flight.

In the meantime, Shara returned to Baghdad to get instructions about what he was to do next. Unbeknownst to Shara or Coddling, the CIA had had Shara under surveillance for the previous four weeks. How the CIA knew about Shara could not be determined. Apparently, the agency had an Arab informant living in Athens who had been friendly with him. It was also likely that British intelligence had found out about a suspicious trip by a British national. Whatever the case, the CIA determined conclusively that a bomb was now sitting in Coddling's Athens apartment.

The CIA contacted the Greek foreign intelligence service, known as KYP. It was an intelligence service with which the United States had a special relationship—in 1947, the CIA had founded the KYP and subsidized it secretly for many years. But ever since Prime Minister Andreas Papandreou had come to power in 1981 there had been a lot of hostility toward the United States. Details of the cozy relationship between the U.S. government and the 1974 Greek colonels' dictatorship had been leaking out for some time, so the resentment was still raw. The new regime seemed to bend over backward to help the Soviet Union. Papandreou apparently bore an animosity to the United States that was unforgiving.

With some apparent misgivings, the CIA had notified the KYP about the presence of a bomb in Coddling's apartment. But when Greek intelligence services went in, they could find no bomb—ironically reminiscent of the time that the Swiss federal police had entered Adnan's room in Geneva only to miss that the bomb was contained in his suitcase. The KYP notified the CIA that there was no bomb to find. Whether the Greek inability to retrieve the bomb was deliberate or inadvertent, the United States was not going to wait to find out.

The United States decided then to take matters into its own hands. Weeks after Coddling had returned to Athens with the suitcase, empty but still wired as a bomb, a U.S. attaché—in fact the third-ranking CIA operations officer in Greece—assigned to the United States embassy in Athens, secretly entered Coddling's apartment while she was out. He was joined by a British intelligence officer. They left the apartment with the suitcase bomb.

It was an extraordinary action undertaken by the CIA. Breaking into the apartment was easy—but conducting a covert operation on foreign soil without notifying the host government was risky and politically dangerous. Yet, the CIA station had concluded that it had to act unilaterally for fear that the KYP had somehow been corrupted by Papandreou's people.

Unbeknownst to the CIA and to the British MI-6, a Greek intelligence officer had been posted to conduct twenty-four-hour surveillance on Coddling's apartment. The agent observed the American-British intelligence team enter the apartment and leave with a suitcase.

Greece did not let on to the fact that it had witnessed the American covert operation, waiting instead to see what the United States would do.

The United States then warned the Greek government that Shara was a member of a terrorist group and that if he entered Greece again, he should be arrested. The Greeks were given copies of Shara's passport. On April 16, Shara returned to Athens from Baghdad and was detained at the airport by Greek immigration officials. He was placed in administrative detention in an Athens jail but was not charged with any crime.

American officials asked Greece to hand Shara over to them. Greek officials took their time responding to the request. Then, on May 10, relations between the two countries took a particularly nasty turn. Papandreou, addressing the first congress of his Panhellenic Socialist Movement, declared, "The Soviet Union's fight for détente is genuine. The U.S.S.R. cannot be called an imperialist power like the United States." The next day, a State Department spokesman in Washington blasted the Greek government for "such an outrageous comparison."

Shortly after this unusually acerbic diplomatic exchange, the Greek regime formally notified the United States that it would not even consider Shara's extradition. Instead, the Greek government reserved its rage for the United States: It expelled the American agent who had entered Coddling's apartment.

The United States then asked Greece to put Shara on trial for attempting to bomb the El Al plane. Greek officials asked the United States to hand over the bomb. But U.S. diplomats did not want to surrender possession. It was an incredible intelligence find—it was at least the fifth Abu Ibrahim bomb intercepted intact by the United States, and it would provide FBI explosives experts with a fantastic opportunity to see what changes Abu Ibrahim had been able to make in his "invisible bombs."

Besides wanting to study the bomb for themselves to see how it might have differed from others, American officials were worried that the Papandreou regime might actually return the bomb to Iraq. So, instead of offering to turn it over to Greece, American diplomats began stalling. "We'll give it over in twenty-four hours," was their first response. But they had no intention of doing so. The twenty-four hours stretched into a week. Then the United States leaked a cover story: The bomb had been detonated as it was being dismantled. But "luckily," the United States told the Greeks, agents had taken photos of the bomb before it had "exploded." The United States then offered to provide these pictures. Greek officials refused the offer, saying that evidence collected from a foreign intelligence service could not be used in court. The Greek government publicly declared that the United States was "tampering with evidence and obstruction of justice." American officials felt that Greece was using this excuse as a legal ruse to avoid having to put a Palestinian on trial.

Greek reluctance to press charges against Shara, American officials suspected, stemmed not only from antagonism toward the United States but also from elements of the Greek government who were rabidly pro-PLO. It was a suspicion that would be infuriatingly confirmed.

During the bitter wrangling between the United States and Greece over the affair, American officials learned that within the Greek government, a key official had been orchestrating the case on behalf of Shara. His name was Kostas Tsimas, and he was the chief intelligence adviser to Prime Minister Papandreou.

Tsimas had been an activist in the PASOC party when it was in opposition from 1974 through 1981. During that time, according to Greek sources, Tsimas had been the PASOC party's liaison to the Iraqi Baath party. In that capacity, he had served as Iraq's eyes and ears in Greece. He had traveled extensively throughout the Middle East, including an unusual visit to PLO camps in Lebanon. As he rose to positions of influence in the Papandreou regime—later he would become the head of the Greek intelligence service—he increasingly used his power to protect Arab and Palestinian terrorists.

In late May 1984, about five weeks after he had been arrested, Shara was released from jail and flown, all expenses paid, to Algiers. From there, he made his way back to Baghdad, where he joined up again with Abu Ibrahim. Over the next eighteen months, through late 1985, Shara carried out more than half a dozen bombings around the world, including one in Singapore in 1985 at the office building housing the Israeli embassy.

10

Life in America

Adnan found that his dream of life in America collided with hard reality in Miami. The most obvious discrepancy was that Jerry Lewis and Dean Martin weren't his neighbors, not everyone drove a 1956 Plymouth convertible, and democracy didn't mean that Adnan had the freedom to do whatever he pleased.

Somehow he could never accept that his experience was not going to be like the movies. Although it was initially exciting, he was increasingly annoyed by the heavy security that preempted his every move.

Accompanied by U.S. marshals, Adnan flew from Washington, D.C., to Miami on November 22, 1984. He was taken to the "Tower," the U.S. courthouse on North Miami Avenue. First on the agenda was giving him yet another identity. Since leaving Baghdad, Adnan had been assigned three: Mohammed Jassin Khalaf, Mario Rosatti, and Mahmod al-Altie. It was a sensitive subject.

Adnan had a hard time dealing with the odd sensations that followed such a dehumanizing process. "I feel my name. I am proud of my name and my family," he said.

"Whatever name I carry now I have no attachment to."

He wasn't given long to mull over the choices and the Witness Protection Program was not terribly compassionate. The program wasn't designed to deal with problems relating to culture shock. This was a simple transaction to them, not an emotional issue. And it certainly wasn't a good time, as far as they were concerned, to have an identity crisis. Adnan deliberated. "I thought I should pick a name that would be very friendly to Americans," he says. "I chose an Egyptian one because the Americans liked the Egyptians and were at peace with them."

He became Sammy Sharif, hoping that identification with the dashing actor Omar Sharif would make him more appealing.

The Federal Witness Protection Program was established two decades ago primarily to protect American witnesses testifying against organized-crime operatives—but it has dramatically expanded its scope. Working in conjunction with the Justice Department's Criminal Division, the U.S. Marshals Service has been responsible for administering the program. In 1990, 173 witnesses (not counting their families) were admitted. As of March 1, 1991, that brought to 5,686 the number of witnesses admitted since the program's inception in 1971. Once a witness enters the program, the marshals' protection is a lifetime guarantee. Though the program does not provide details regarding the background of their members, it is known that only a rare few are not United States citizens. Sammy Sharif was one of those few.

While deciding what they would do with him, the marshals assigned a woman police officer to show him around. She didn't understand Arabic and he barely spoke English but somehow she knew that Adnan was dying to see the beach. They drove there and he got out of the car. It was chilly but it could never compare to the biting cold of the Swiss Alps. The waves crashed on the shore. He smiled as he felt the wind whipping through his hair and tasted the salt on his lips. This was where he wanted to be.

The police officer asked him if he was hungry. She took him to a diner, where he ordered some kind of sandwich that he had never had before. The most mundane necessities, like eating, were becoming cultural odysseys. At the end of the meal the officer insisted on paying. "This got me very upset," Adnan said. "It isn't the custom in my country and I told her I didn't need a lady with a gun to protect me." Such conflicts between Adnan and his U.S. caretakers would become routine.

The two made amends and returned to the Tower. The marshals had arranged for Adnan to stay in their holding cell in the basement (the very same place Manuel Noriega was detained five years later). The accommodations were certainly adequate but Adnan felt like a prisoner. The classified area had been nicknamed the "Submarine" because it had no windows and the pipes ran along the ceiling of the passageway.

Adnan was a hero, not a criminal. He had saved lives, not destroyed them. He had accepted an invitation to come to the United States to help the American people. He wasn't obligated. Yet the stifling treatment—between the high security and living underground—was too much to handle. It didn't seem fair. He complained to the marshals, who agreed to move him to the Everglades Hotel, in the downtown district of Miami.

He didn't last long at the Everglades either. The main problem was finding food. He had learned about hamburgers in Washington but everything else was a mystery. He wanted hummos and there didn't seem to be any in Miami. The clincher was the day he walked out of his hotel and saw a little umbrella, a man and a food cart. "Maybe," he thought, "there will be something for me." But when the man explained he was selling hot dogs, Adnan was horrified. Sickened. He'd been subjected to a lot of nasty things in the PLO but *never* had they forced him to eat dog.

He moved out of his hotel a day later in search of a place he could stay that had a kitchen. From now on, he decided, he'd prepare his meals himself.

The doorman at the hotel had made a suggestion—Adnan's only requirements were that it have a kitchenette and be inexpensive—and, after his shift, the doorman gave him a lift to a motel along Biscayne Boulevard.

Things started looking up. Lots of women apparently lived at the motel and they all were exceedingly friendly. As he was sitting on his balcony, one waved and suggested that she come over to meet him. "Sure," Adnan said. He gave her a drink. There wasn't a lot to talk about—his vocabulary was seriously limited—but this woman was skilled in the universal language of love. Twenty dollars was all it would cost. Such a proposition was hard to refuse. So hard, in fact, that Adnan didn't turn two other women away that day either.

The next morning his conscience nagged him. The U.S. government was trying their best. He ought to at least let them know that he was all right—even if he did hate the hotel they originally found for him. There wasn't a phone in his room so he went down to the lobby and made a call to the local marshal's office to say that he'd left the Everglades.

"Where are you?" the marshal asked, trying to sound nonchalant.

"I don't know," Adnan said.

"Is there someone there who does?" the marshal asked, now clearly agitated.

Adnan got the owner of the motel to pick up the phone and give the marshal the address.

Adnan went back to relaxing on his balcony and was a little taken aback when, a few minutes later, three undercover cars came screeching to a halt down below. They got his things together and insisted he leave with them.

"This is the red-light district!" they said. "You could have been killed."

They coaxed Adnan into staying at the Everglades again. It was the holiday season and he was acutely aware of his solitary existence. On New Year's Eve he saw how happy the people were outside of his hotel. He closed the curtains and went to bed before dark. "I didn't even cry when my mother died," he said. "But now the tears flowed like a river."

Living in Switzerland had been stressful—compared to the ease he would have had living anywhere in the Middle East—but it didn't come close to the tension he felt in the United States. At least in Europe, speaking several languages was common; people were familiar with many different cultures. But in the United States, the Arab world was too removed. The sight of a Palestinian in Florida struck most people as bizarre.

Soon the marshals had arranged for him to live in an apartment in Miami Beach. He was sent to Berlitz to learn English and they gave him a stipend: $2,000 to buy a car and $900 a month to live on. It was a paltry sum compared to what the Swiss had provided. "I bought a used Cadillac," Adnan said. "It was a piece of junk. I just couldn't live comfortably with what they gave me."

Though he tried not to think about what could have been, every once in a while he weakened. He spent days dreaming about the millions he once had in the bank and the cars with thousands of dollars stashed under the front seat. He had always been able to make something of himself, no matter how hard the circumstances were, but this cultural abyss was proving to be unbridgeable. A component of the Witness Protection Program is assisting the witness in becoming self-sufficient. A national job bank is at the program's disposal. But Adnan was a hard person to place. He could neither read nor write English and, though he was an engineer by training, he had no degree. The marshals turned up one possibility. It was to be a mechanic at a school, making less than $10 an hour. "Imagine, a millionaire working as a mechanic," Adnan thought. "And this is supposed to be the land where dreams come true." Even though he was willing to humble himself and take the job, he was denied it because of his illiteracy. The marshals, he said, never attempted to find him employment again. Had he known how tough it was going to be, he often thought to himself, he would have gladly endured the coldest winters in Switzerland.

Angry, depressed, and alone, Adnan didn't know what to do with himself—until Millie entered his life. They met at a piano bar. He told her that he was an engineer. They talked a lot that night and she wound up giving him a ride home and her phone number.

They quickly fell in love.

Millie worked as the secretary to the Costa Rican consul in Miami. Besides her official job, she made private travel arrangements for Costa Rican President Luis Alberto Monge and his wife, Doris. The twist was that they usually came at separate times to visit their respective lovers.

With Millie, Adnan's social circle widened. The group included intriguing people who were usually embroiled in some sort of scandal. President Monge and his girlfriend often dined with them. When the first lady was in town visiting her boyfriend, José Luis Rodriguez, they'd double-date. Millie told Adnan that Rodriguez was a popular balladeer who went by the stage name "El Puma," and that—on the sly—Mrs. Monge had financed Rodriguez's failed attempt to run for president of Venezuela.

Adnan had been impatient for his independence, and his relationship with Millie made him feel as though he had regained control. He told her of his true background. It didn't make a difference to her. As their love grew, so too did the desire for commitment. It was more Millie's wish than Adnan's, but he certainly wasn't reluctant. She spoke of his moving to Costa Rica with her, and it all sounded swell. The only problem, Adnan said, was that the American government had not been able to issue him a passport yet.

Millie was undaunted. As a member of the diplomatic staff and close friend of the president and his wife, a passport for her husband would not be hard to arrange.

He called the marshals to tell them of his plans. They were stunned. When they recovered, they said that it was not plausible—he didn't possess a passport.

"I told them I didn't need them to get it for me because Millie was going to," he said.

Suddenly their attitude shifted. They had probably counted on stalling him by saying they would put through a request for his passport, never intending to do so. Now they had to actually confront the issue. The marshal he spoke with in Miami said that Adnan's request would have to be cleared through Washington. So Adnan went to Washington. There, the marshals asked who the woman was. He explained that she worked for the consul of Costa Rica and was a friend of the ambassador. "I told them and they said, 'Fine.'" Adnan remembers. "They only asked that Millie not get involved with the passport situation. 'We'll deal with that,' they said."

But by the time Adnan got back to Miami, things had changed. A marshal was waiting at his apartment.

"You have to move," he said.

"What are you talking about?" Adnan asked, bewildered. "I have a lover here who I'm going to marry. Why would I move?" It was August 1986; Adnan had been living there for only nine months.

"You're in danger," the marshal said.

The U.S. Marshals Service had him shipped out of Miami Beach in less than forty-eight hours. They instructed him not to call anybody, saying it was for his own good. They wouldn't even tell him where he was going. "I believed them," Adnan said. "I thought they knew something that I didn't."

Adnan was just beginning to realize that there was a huge flaw in the Witness Protection Program: It didn't allow for human relationships.

"I was alone in a strange country, I didn't speak the language, I didn't have any friends, and still I worried about my safety," Adnan said. "All this because of a bomb I didn't want and my willingness to help."

He started all over again in another city. His name became Joe (which is the alias he uses with all reporters). It was a much colder climate than Miami but the consolation was that it had a larger Arab community.

After about four months, he met an Arab woman who had been living in the United States for over twenty years. She had a successful business and didn't question Adnan—she just enjoyed his company. It was an enormous release for him to be among his own people. While he couldn't share his secrets, he at least had the language to convey his thoughts.

Adnan was still part of the Witness Protection Program, but had heard nothing of Mohammed Rashid in the two years since his arrival in Florida. He had been told that the whole case would take only a year—but his recent dealings with the U.S. marshals had taught him never to trust what they said. Still he had no passport, still he had not served as a witness against Rashid, and still they insisted everything was fine. It made him sick.

At the same time, his old boss, Abu Ibrahim, was experiencing difficulties of his own. In fact, by 1985, the May 15 Organization was suffering deep internal turmoil. As Adnan knew all too well, Ibrahim ruled the May 15 Organization with such an iron hand that many of his operatives had become paranoid. Even Ibrahim himself had become paranoid. But as Dashiell Hammett once wryly noted, even paranoids have enemies. In Abu Ibrahim's case, it was becoming abundantly clear that concerns about having enemies were justified. In nearly all of his operations against airplanes over the previous two years, something had gone wrong. It must have seemed to him that informants had thoroughly penetrated his group.

First Shara had been arrested and the bomb he made was confiscated by an American intelligence agent. Then, in June 1984, another operation went sour. A month earlier—even as Shara was being held by the Greeks—

Ibrahim planned another attack on El Al Airlines. He manufactured two suitcase bombs, each loaded with nearly a kilogram of Semtex. The explosives, in typical fashion, were cut into thin, eight-by-twelve-inch sheets, which were then sewn into the membrane of each suitcase's lining. Ibrahim arranged for a courier to transport the suitcases to East Berlin. Then the courier crossed the border into West Berlin and headed for an apartment in the American sector.

Once he crossed the border, however, the courier was placed under surveillance by Mossad agents. They tracked him to the apartment, where he dropped off his cargo and left. A month before, an informant had tipped the Mossad off to a possible operation by Ibrahim to be launched from West Berlin. Israeli agents began a surveillance operation aimed at suspected members of the May 15 Organization, which put them on the lookout for a courier crossing the border from East Berlin. Their informant had told them that El Al had been targeted, and that a bomb would be smuggled aboard an airliner in Berlin on its way to Tel Aviv.

After concluding that the cargo the courier had dropped off was likely to be the bomb they were looking for, the Mossad contacted the West Berlin police, who raided the apartment on June 25. Two Palestinians were arrested, and both admitted working for Abu Ibrahim. Later that year, the West German government expelled the men, who made their way back to Baghdad.

Despite his failures, Abu Ibrahim continued to work diligently on achieving what obviously had been a lifelong goal: downing an airplane in midair. But, again, he was frustrated. On November 7, 1984, West German authorities pulled a young Palestinian man out of line after he presented his Tunisian passport to airline officials. The man had already purchased a ticket to fly on Lufthansa to Athens. But West German officials were on the lookout for certain passport holders. Closer scrutiny of the man's passport proved the officials' suspicions to be correct: It was forged. Security forces then inspected the man's carry-on baggage. Two and a half pounds of Semtex were found. The man was an Abu Ibrahim courier.

As disappointing as these failed terrorist attacks must have been for Abu Ibrahim, they were becoming even more of a problem for his Iraqi benefactors. His terrorist acts had been so poorly disguised that he was becoming a liability to the Iraqi government.

Adnan's story was still fresh in the files of several Western intelligence services; Ibrahim's activities were duly noted by the CIA and the British, and the Israelis in particular had kept track of the terrorist, often protesting bitterly in private that American policy toward Iraq was encouraging the very things that CIA operations officers were trying to stop. There was also growing evidence of other terrorists besides Ibrahim who claimed Iraq as a patron. Abu Abbas, whose operatives, in October 1985, would hijack the *Achille Lauro* cruise ship, murdering a wheelchair-bound American passenger, had received plenty of financial and logistical support from Saddam Hussein. In fact, Abu Abbas was given an Iraqi diplomatic passport, which he used to his great advantage in freely traveling around Europe. Abu Nidal had also been given assistance by Iraq, but on a more sporadic basis. Samir Gousha of the Palestine Liberation Front and Arafat's secret terror branch, Force 17, were routinely given weapons and money.

In various meetings in Washington and in Baghdad, American intelligence officials had let Iraqi officials know that they were fully aware that Ibrahim and Saddam's other terrorists continued to be very active—notwithstanding the public declarations of the State Department. To keep American pressure off, Iraqi officials, recalled American intelligence sources, had pressed Ibrahim to cover up any connection between his operations and Iraq. At the same time, Iraqi officials had repeatedly been telling the Americans that Ibrahim was no longer in business. But now it was time for Ibrahim to "disband"—and persuade the Americans that this time it was for real.

For Abu Ibrahim, there would be one last effort to carry out a mass murder against the Israelis or Americans. On October 15, 1985, two couriers were dispatched on Iraqi Airways to Rome. According to American intelligence officials, they were waved through regular security at Baghdad International Airport. In their possession were two suitcases, each containing 7.7 pounds of plastic explosives. Once they arrived in Rome, their mission was to smuggle the suitcases aboard either El Al planes or American aircraft. If that failed, they were to try to destroy Israeli or Jewish targets. But at the airport in Rome, one of the men was detained when he presented his false Moroccan passport to immigration officials. The passport said he was Ben Krami, age twenty-three.

Italian immigration officials had stopped the man because there was something suspicious about the passport. Now airport security police decided to examine his brownish-red suitcase. When the suitcase was opened, all that could be seen were clothes. Officials emptied the suitcase of its contents, then weighed it. The scale showed it to be unusually heavy—too heavy to be totally empty. Further inspection revealed a false bottom containing the 7.7 pounds of explosives.

Police immediately reviewed the passenger list and found that the man had traveled to Rome with another. The second man was apprehended a short time later as he headed downtown on the airport shuttle bus. His suitcase bomb was retrieved by Italian police from a locker in the central train station.

In response to the announcement by Italian police that they had arrested two Iraqis with bombs after they arrived on Iraqi Airways, *The Washington Post* quoted an Iraqi spokesman in Washington saying that the Italian police reports were "definitely not true. . . . We would never allow that." He accused the stories of being planted by unidentified people who were "poisoning U.S.-Iraqi relations." The State Department response to the Italian reports was not that much better than Iraq's: In press briefings, State refused to comment at all. But privately, American intelligence and Justice Department officials at the CIA were livid—not only at the Iraqis but at the State Department as well.

It was not long after that Iraq's terrorist connections were exposed once again, with the *Achille Lauro* hijacking. The twenty-three-thousand-ton seven-deck cruise liner was commandeered thirty miles off the coast of Port Said, Egypt, by a group of heavily armed Palestinian terrorists belonging to the Palestine Liberation Front. At the time, eighty passengers were on board; some eight hundred others had elected to disembark to visit Cairo and the Pyramids. The hijackers broadcast their demands: Unless Israel released fifty Palestinian terrorists from Israeli prisons, they would blow up the 624-foot vessel.

In a drama played out to the horror of the entire world,

which watched and listened to news reports, the terrorists executed an American invalid, Leon Klinghoffer. Two days later, the terrorists gave themselves up after their leader, Abu Abbas, arrived from an unknown location in the Middle East and personally negotiated a deal with Egypt that guaranteed the terrorists free passage from Egypt. Iraq had secretly agreed to give them sanctuary. American jets intercepted the plane carrying the terrorists to freedom, forcing it to land in Italy, where they were arrested. Abu Abbas was also arrested, but was suddenly let go by the Italians. His first stop was Belgrade, Yugoslavia. Though the State Department publicly professed at the time not to know where Abbas had gone after that, American intelligence tracked him to Baghdad, where he was given refuge. In fact, Abbas had been given a diplomatic passport by Iraq.

In Baghdad, however, Iraqi officials must surely have been concerned—not only because of Abbas's presence but because of the Iraqi fingerprints left by Abu Ibrahim's operatives when they were caught with the bombs in Rome. Iraq was all too aware of growing pressure in the United States Congress to put Iraq back on the list of countries supporting terrorism. The previous June, in a letter to Congressman Howard Berman, who had complained about Iraqi-supported terrorism, Secretary of State George Shultz wrote that if the State Department found that "any group based in or supported by Iraq is engaged in terrorist acts, we would promptly return Iraq to the list of countries identified as supporting terrorism."

By January 1986 congressional pressure to restore Iraq to the terrorism list had reached such a height that Operation Sub-Group, an interagency anti-terrorism committee, met at the White House to discuss the issue. National Security Council aide Lt. Col. Oliver North was present at the meeting; ironically, it was he who had been a strong proponent of the administration's decision to provide satellite intelligence to the Iraqis on Iranian troop formations. At the meeting, according to classified documents obtained by the Iran-contra congressional committee, it was noted that evidence of Iraqi support for Abu Ibrahim and Abu Abbas could jeopardize the special relationship with Iraq under which American satellite intelligence was being provided to Baghdad.

Iraq knew something had to be done. It was now time to make Abu Ibrahim "disappear"—or at least make the Americans believe so. Would the United States buy the story? That was the question. One person who could help provide the answer was Adnan, who was still the country's most important source on the Abu Ibrahim organization.

11

Ibrahim's Legacy

Iraq vowed that all terrorism would be stopped. But on April 2, 1986, both Iraq and American intelligence officials knew that the Iraqis had duped the United States.

Descending to ten thousand feet, the Trans World Airlines Boeing 727 from Rome was on its final approach to the Athens airport when there was an explosion that created a massive hole in the right side of the fuselage. Due to the decompression, four passengers were sucked out of the hole. Later examination by Denny Kline of the FBI showed that the bomb had been placed under the cushion in seat 10F.

The hole created by the explosion was nearly five by six feet. The legs and lower torso of the passenger sitting in 10F were extensively mutilated. He died immediately. The three other victims were sucked out of the plane alive. A medical report would later note that they died from the force of hitting the ground.

As horrible and gruesome as these deaths were, it was a miracle that there were not more casualties. "There was a big bang and then the man beside me was blown out along with his seat," passenger Ibrahim al-Nami told *The New York Times.* "I felt myself being pulled out, too, and I hung on to my wife's seat beside me."

Had the blast occurred at a higher altitude, the loss of cabin pressure would have caused the entire plane to explode, much like a filled balloon when a needle punctures its skin.

Of the four passengers who sat in row 10, three were Greek-Americans from a small city in Annapolis, Maryland, three generations of the same family: fifty-two-year-old Demetra Stylian, her twenty-four-year-old daughter, Maria Klug, and Maria's nine-month-old daughter, Demetra. The fourth victim, the man who sat in 10F, was thirty-nine-year-old Alberto Ospino of Stratford, Connecticut. Three of the bodies were recovered on the ground near the town of Argos. The fourth was found in the sea.

Claim for the attack came from a group not previously very active, the Lebanese-based Arab Revolutionary Cells. A report at the time said it was part of the renegade Abu Nidal group.

In fact, according to U.S. intelligence officials, the attack was orchestrated by a terrorist anointed by Abu Ibrahim as his successor, Abdullah Labib, the head of a new organization called the Hawari Apparatus.

Intelligence authorities say that Hawari essentially assumed most of the infrastructure of the Abu Ibrahim group. "In reality," recalled Denny Kline, "it was the May 15 Organization operating under another name." Abu Ibrahim's too-high visibility had required him to "disappear," but his entire terrorist infrastructure—bombs, safe houses, couriers—was 100 percent intact. Everyone, including Mohammed Rashid and Fouad Hussein

Shara, was now secretly integrated into the Hawari Apparatus. Again, like at other momentous times in the underground battle by counterterrorist officials, Adnan was left out in the cold.

Labib was better known as Colonel Hawari, in part because of his physical similarity to the popular and charismatic Algerian president, Houari Boumedienne. Boumedienne assumed power in 1965 after he engineered the overthrow of Ahmed Ben Bella.

Besides being connected to Iraq, the Hawari Apparatus was also tied to the PLO Fatah. According to a Defense Department document, when the Hawari Apparatus assumed operational control of the Abu Ibrahim organization, it had already established itself as the clandestine terror arm of the PLO's Fatah, known as Fatah's Special Operations Group. Working directly under PLO leader Yasser Arafat, Hawari had been secretly appointed by Arafat in the early 1980s to assume operational control over Fatah's Special Operations. This gave Arafat the "plausible deniabily" he needed in denying any connection to international terrorism.

In his first two years, Hawari targeted Syrian forces in Lebanon as well as those belonging to Abu Musa, a renegade Palestinian working on behalf of the Syrians. Hawari carried out multiple bombings against Syrian army positions in Beirut and elsewhere in Lebanon.

Though in the 1970s, Fatahs Special Operations was headquartered in Beirut, it relocated with PLO chairman Arafat to Tunis in 1982. After the move, Arafat decided to establish several clandestine terror branches to carry out attacks, but which would operate at an "arm's length" distance. Hawari carried out terrorist attacks under the secret control of Arafat. Recalled Vince Cannistraro, former head of counterterrorism for the CIA, "We had indisputable intelligence showing that Arafat was continuing to orchestrate terrorism through Hawari but publicly continuing to utter the words the West wanted to hear."

Following the devastating 1985 Israeli attack on PLO headquarters—after another secret Arafat group, Force 17, executed Israeli tourists in Cyprus—Tunisia would no longer allow Arafat to openly use Tunis as a base. Iraq, according to American and Israeli intelligence officials, invited Arafat to come and set up a secret base within its borders. Hawari, working for both Abu Ibrahim and Arafat, became the head of the "new" organization—though what had in fact happened was that Arafat simply was able to acquire another clandestine terror branch. The ease with which Arafat was able to gain control over the Abu Ibrahim organization has led American intelligence officials to suspect that all along Abu Ibrahim might have been working in tandem with him in carrying out the terror attacks from 1980 through 1985.

The emergence and proliferation of different names and groups associated with Hawari's group was meant to disguise the bottom line: The Iraqis had simply reconstituted the May 15 Organization under a new name and new leader, thus allowing them to insist to the State Department that Abu Ibrahim had been "retired."

American and Greek investigators traced the bomb on the TWA plane to the person who had occupied seat 10F when the jet had flown from Cairo to Athens earlier that day. From the manifest, the passenger was identified as May Elias Mansur from Tripoli, Lebanon. In response to being named in news reports as a possible suspect, Mansur held a press conference in Tripoli. She denied she had had anything to do with the bombing: "I don't undertake such crimes that kill innocent people and children." But she added, "I support attacks on U.S. embassies and installations," and launched into a bitter tirade against Jews and the United States. Though Mansur has remained a prime suspect to this day, intelligence officials believe that Mohammed Rashid was involved in transporting the bomb to the last courier who brought it onto the plane. According to evidence collected by American intelligence officials, Rashid is believed to have transported the bomb from Baghdad in the weeks before the explosion.

Intelligence officials were later able to conclude with near 100 percent certainty that the Hawari Apparutus had carried out the attack. The signature of the bomb, aviation and explosive experts discovered, was identical to those of the bombs manufactured by Abu Ibrahim. According to former FAA official Billy Vincent, the "bomb had an electric timer and a barometric sensor. . . . The bomb is thought to have been identical to the device that exploded on the Pan Am B-747 on August 11, 1982, and the bomb found on the Pan Am B-747 on August 25, 1982."

Though Ibrahim had officially left the scene, his diabolical technology was being put to good use. His home in Baghdad continued to be used to create bombs. Key operatives, including Rashid, were dispatched from Baghdad to cities in Europe and Asia, to conduct surveillance for future terrorist attacks and to recruit unwitting dupes.

Shara was sent to Tunisia to work directly with Arafat's Fatah, and from there, he was sent to Lebanon, where he was supposed to carry out terror attacks against Syria, Iraq's longtime foe. But in Lebanon, Christian forces, for reasons still unclear, arrested him in April 1987. He was held in jail until September 1990. Then he made his way to the coastal city of Sidon, purchased a false passport for $300, and headed by ferry to Cyprus. Shara had been on the Mossad's most-wanted list since he had been released by Greece after attempting to blow up the El Al aircraft in late 1983. Alerted by the Mossad, Israeli naval forces intercepted the ferry, arrested Shara, and brought him back to Israel, where he is now being held.

In March 1987, seven members of a cell working for Colonel Hawari were arrested in Paris. In their possession, French police found a large cache of weapons, including grenades, explosives, automatic pistols, and submachine guns. A year later, the seven were convicted by a French court. In addition, the court sentenced Colonel Hawari in absentia to a ten-year term for his participation in the plot to smuggle arms into France. There was simply no doubt among investigators that Iraq had played a key role in helping the Hawari cell acquire its weapons in France.

The State Department continued to whitewash this persistent evidence of ongoing Iraqi support for terrorism. But in the State Department's Office for Combatting Terrorism, there was deep frustration at U.S. policy. Though officials were institutionally forced to support the general policy, internally there were no illusions about the degree of Iraqi support for terrorism. "There were essentially three problems that we had with the Iraqis by 1986," recalled Ambassador L. Paul Bremer III, the head of the Office for Combatting Terrorism from 1986 through 1989. "One, the Iraqis were still using terrorism against Iraqi dissidents; two, they had given refuge to Abu Abbas, who was the mastermind of the *Achille Lauro* hijacking; and three, they had the May 15 group present in Baghdad."

In his official capacity, Bremer would hold his own meetings with foreign officials to discuss terrorism. When he brought up their support for terrorism, Bremer said that the response of Iraqi officials was deafening: "The Iraqi government basically listened and said nothing. . . . They basically didn't have a defense, saying, 'Abu Abbas is not a terrorist' or 'Abu Ibrahim isn't here.' They just listened. It was a stonewall. . . . It was just a complete stonewall."

With total impunity, Iraq had openly backed Abbas and reconstituted Ibrahim's into a new organization. "We weren't fooled by what Iraq was doing," recalled Denny Kline, the man on the receiving end of Ibrahim's unexploded and intercepted bombs. (In fact, until he left the FBI's explosives section in 1988, Kline would come across as many as fifteen bombs that had been prepared by Abu Ibrahim.) "Ibrahim was not only a bomb maker but he was a teacher—and he taught his disciples such as Colonel Hawari how to make the same type of bombs." In most of the cases where the bombs were found, either by the United States or more commonly by Israeli and European intelligence services, American officials elected to keep existence of the bombs a secret. But at those levels of the FBI and CIA that dealt with the raw intelligence, there was no doubt that Iraq had allowed and encouraged the proliferation of these invisible bombs. "I was always amazed by the degree to which we took Iraq at its word— the proof of their lies was in my hands," recalled Kline. "I was also amazed at the fact that the government never sufficiently utilized Adnan Awad."

In fact, since coming to the United States in November 1984, Adnan had been effectively quarantined. The one eyewitness to Iraq's terror network had been treated like everyone else in the Federal Witness Protection Program, who were mostly criminals.

Life in an alien country like the United States was difficult enough, but the security restrictions imposed by the U.S. marshals were making things intolerable. American intelligence agencies knew that if Adnan's existence in the United States had leaked out to Abu Ibrahim or to Iraq or to any terrorist group, there would be a concerted effort to have him killed. In fact, one foreign Middle Eastern intelligence service had notified the CIA that Iraqi military intelligence had put a contract on Adnan's head. There was no way of confirming the report, which had come from an informant who the CIA was not able to interview in person, but it raised alarm bells. There was no reason to take any unnecessary risks.

One evening, Adnan received a telephone call from someone who said he was in the CIA. The man said he had a green card for Adnan, something he had been trying to get for a while. But the man sounded a bit nervous on the telephone and Adnan picked up on this. "If you are really from the CIA, why don't you come meet me in person as the government always does when they talk to me?" There was silence on the other end of the phone, then the line went dead. Adnan immediately called the marshals.

Ten minutes later, a marshal showed up at his door. "You must come with us for the night. Now!" Adnan could see that the man was very concerned. He grabbed a shirt and left with the marshal. The next day, the marshals began to investigate the possibility that someone from the CIA may have tried to call him—but they turned up no positive responses. Something was wrong. Someone may have found out about Adnan's existence.

The marshals asked Adnan to relocate again. It was urgent, they told him. But Adnan, who had already moved several times, was tired of picking up, leaving, and starting life anew. He knew that the marshals feared that his life was in danger if he stayed in the same city—but Adnan found himself curiously unconcerned about the threat. He was tired, lonely, emotionally exhausted. He put his foot down. "I'm not leaving," he said. It wasn't that he was ungrateful to the marshals for the protection they provided, just that he was at the breaking point—and he had just started to make some friends in this city.

But the marshals insisted. That evening Adnan told his girlfriend that he had to relocate because of work. She asked if she could move with him. He told her she couldn't. Why? she asked. "Company policy," he said. "Then to hell with company policy!" she shouted back in tears.

Adnan began to think to himself that if he stayed in the Witness Protection Program, he would never be able to give out his phone number or even get married. Adnan thrived on being around people. He was not a loner. He was a gregarious and spontaneous person. Yet the life he had to live was that of a loner. He was miserable. "I decided at that point that unless the FBI could send me to the moon, there was no way I could do what they wanted and remain uninvolved with people."

At the time, Adnan was receiving $1,500 a month from the U.S. government. It paid for his basic necessities but not much else. Certainly, it was nothing at all like the good old days when he was an extravagant spender and could carouse all night. Adnan decided to tell the marshals that he was not going to relocate. He had made his decision and would not change it.

Upon learning of Adnan's decision, the marshals were taken aback. They told Adnan that if he disobeyed the Witness Protection Program's requirements, he would have to leave it and that the marshals would no longer be responsible for his safety. Adnan knew that would happen—and said he was prepared for that possibility. The marshals asked him to sign an agreement that legally released them of all obligations.

Life took a new turn for Adnan. He started a little business with his girlfriend, and even moved in with her. For the first time since he had arrived in the United States, he felt good about himself. His girlfriend helped give him a new self-confidence. She even suggested that he start an import business so that he wouldn't have to rely on English so much. Adnan was delighted by the prospect of finally starting life anew.

Not long after, he got a call from Dan Bent, the U.S. attorney from Hawaii, who said he wanted to visit. Adnan was pleased to hear from his old friend, whom he hadn't seen since first coming to the United States. When Bent showed up at his meager home, Adnan welcomed him enthusiastically. After a while, Bent came out with the reason why he had made the visit. "Do you still want to help us?" he asked Adnan as if he thought Adnan might have changed his mind.

Adnan nodded his head. "Of course I do. I came to this country because I believe in human life." Bent thanked him profusely and then left.

12

The Indictment

Meanwhile, Adnan's old acquaintance Mohammed Rashid was the subject of increasingly intense scrutiny in Washington, D.C.

"The first time I ever heard of Mohammed Rashid was my very first day on the job in 1984 as the deputy assistant attorney general," recalled Victoria Toensing.

Toensing, then age forty-two, had been appointed in charge of anti-terrorism for the Justice Department after serving as chief counsel for the U.S. Senate Intelligence Committee. But other than having identified Rashid as the person who planted the bomb on board Pan Am Flight 830, the Rashid case file was pretty thin. Clearly, once Rashid had been identified, the legal momentum of the case had come to a standstill. The problem was that the CIA, FBI, and Justice Department all had conflicting institutional interests. Whereas the CIA wanted to collect intelligence yet not jeopardize its sources, the Justice Department wanted prosecutable cases—which required sources to openly identify themselves and be willing to testify. At the FBI, only a few people were pushing the case aggressively. One of them was William Gilman, then a special agent in charge of the counterterrorist section. Another was explosives expert Denny Kline. Moreover, the State Department was still actively suppressing any aggressive counterterrorist investigation into Iraq's ties to Abu Ibrahim.

Bureaucratically, there was nothing career-enhancing about bucking State Department policy and embarrassing one of the Reagan administration's strategic cornerstones. By the time Toensing assumed her post in March 1984, the Rashid case could easily have died. And no one would have cared. Even before Toensing could push the Rashid case, she had to build cooperative interagency relationships that would result in the FBI, CIA, and Justice Department working in harmony rather than at cross purposes.

A strikingly attractive red-haired woman who looked at least ten years her junior, Toensing did not look like the stereotypical terrorist-buster. But if there was anyone who possessed a strong enough sense of determination to see that the Ibrahim case was aggressively pursued, it was Toensing.

A 1962 graduate of Indiana University, Toensing had at first elected not to go to law school. "When I graduated, a woman who was in law school told me of the bitter harassment she was forced to suffer," Toensing recalled. "I didn't want to endure the same humiliation." Toensing ended up raising three children and teaching English part-time, all the while regretting not having gone to law school. One day, she decided she didn't want to kick herself in the shins for the rest of her life. By now divorced, she applied and was accepted to the University of Detroit Law School, where she graduated, cum laude, in

1975. She served for a number of years as assistant U.S. attorney, prosecuting federal narcotics cases.

Toensing met her second husband, Joseph DiGenova, at the 1980 Republican national convention in Detroit. A leader in the Michigan Republican party's Equal Rights Amendment forces, Toensing was selling ERA-GOP pins when DiGenova, a delegate, offered to buy all thirty pins in her inventory. DiGenova would shortly become the U.S. attorney in Washington D.C. Together, Toensing and DiGenova formed what social Washington likes to call a "power couple."

As chief counsel to the Senate Intelligence Committee, Toensing had been in the loop when the United States got hit in Lebanon with the worst terrorist attacks since the days of World War II. First, the American embassy was attacked on April 18, 1983. Sixty-three people lost their lives, including the CIA's chief of station Robert Ames. On October 23 of that same year, the marine barracks was blown up by a suicide truck bomber, killing 241 marines. From Toensing's briefings and close-up involvement in reviewing the intelligence community's files on terrorism, it was easy to see that terrorists were getting away with murder.

"I came in with the mentality that we were going to go after terrorists, whether or not the system was ready." In fact, the system was all *but* ready. When Toensing arrived, the Justice Department was not structured, legally or politically, to handle terrorist investigations. There was a question about where terrorist cases would be tried—in John Martin's internal security unit, which handled espionage cases, or in the General Litigation Department, handled by Toensing. That question was decided in favor of Toensing's shop. Then there was the fact that the FBI under William Webster was not thrilled about the legislation being advanced on Capitol Hill that would give the FBI and Justice Department extra authority to try cases in which Americans were attacked overseas. Though they didn't express it publicly, the FBI leadership did not want the responsibilities that came with extraterritorial jurisdiction.

Besides being generally unprepared to handle counterterrorist investigations, Toensing was facing several cases that required her immediate attention, such as the allegations that there was possible corruption in the investigation of defense contractors on multibillion-dollar ship contracts. Then there was the congressional debate over the landmark 1984 crime bill, which gave prosecutors additional legal powers. Appearing on local television and radio shows, Toensing crisscrossed the country for four months trying to mobilize public opinion in support of the bill.

Daniel Bent, the U.S. district attorney in Hawaii, had been in charge of the Pan Am Flight 830 case since the bombing occurred in 1982. He had interviewed Adnan at length and knew the importance of his testimony in any court case involving Rashid.

For Bent and other attorneys who worked on the case, it had been a nightmare trying to work out of Hawaii. Every other agency whose input would be required—the FBI, FAA, CIA—was located in the Washington area. So an agreement was reached with Toensing to change the venue of the case to Washington, though Bent would continue to take a leading role.

For Toensing, the investigation into Rashid and other terrorists had personal reverberations. "When I came aboard and started learning about the techniques and the fact that it was very difficult to detect bombs, I found myself on my next few flights looking under my seat to see if there was some white or black kind of powder. After a while, you just adjust to it and realize that's the way life is—and it's pure luck whether you happen to be on one of those airplanes. If you start being fearful, then you've let the terrorists win."

Rashid, in the meantime, kept popping up in intelligence reports. Based on reports from informants, among the countries he'd been sighted in were Sudan, West Germany, Tunisia, and Greece. Ironically, because of his active traveling, one FBI official recalled, Rashid was responsible for planting the idea in the minds of FBI and CIA agents that he was "gettable." There had been consideration given on several occasions to snatching Rashid in a covert operation and bringing him back to the United States to stand trial, but those schemes were never developed with Justice Department concurrence.

Toensing's first and foremost concern was making sure that the legal case against Rashid would stick. Until then it had rested primarily on the account of an anonymous informant living in Switzerland. Other than his assumed name, Toensing didn't know anything about the informant. He hadn't been contacted in two years. She didn't even know if he was still around. If he was available, could he serve as a dependable witness? How would he fare on the witness stand? Was he, in fact, reliable? Would he even agree to testify?

Toensing asked the CIA about the mystery man in Switzerland and was told that he was reliable and truthful. But as a prosecutor, Toensing could not take their word. It was not that she didn't trust the CIA, but as a trial lawyer, only she could determine the mystery witness's veracity. Recalled Toensing, "We needed to verify his trustworthiness for ourselves—we needed to be sure that the facts he had relayed to our intelligence agencies would stand up to rigorous cross-examination."

It was then that Dan Bent and other Justice Department officials flew to Geneva to meet Adnan. It didn't take them much time to see for themselves that the prospective witness remembered dates and places with uncanny detail.

Under a little-known law that allows the Central Intelligence Agency director or the attorney general to bring in aliens to the United States and waive immigration procedures, Adnan was brought to the United States. The law, which is rarely invoked, even allows instant naturalization if the person is deemed to have "made an extraordinary contribution to the national security of the United States or the conduct of United States intelligence activities." There was no doubt that Adnan had made such a contribution to U.S. national security. The only question was whether he could make the legal case against Rashid and Abu Ibrahim.

"The witness checked out," recalled Toensing, "and we were pretty sure we had a decent witness." But when she reviewed the FBI interviews, Toensing realized there was a problem. Initial interviews with the passengers and crew on board Pan Am Flight 830 had not been properly done; either the responses had not been properly recorded or the right questions had not been asked. Perhaps the deficiencies in the FBI interviews were understandable in light of the FBI's lack of experience conducting counterterrorist investigations. Nevertheless, from a prosecutorial point of view, the Rashid case was in shambles, and it had to be reconstructed. So FBI agents were dispatched again to track down the passengers who had been on the flight and reinterview them. Agents traveled to Hawaii, California, Texas, and Japan to retake statements. Even the Ozawa family had to be questioned, forced to relive the terrible pain and horror they had experienced.

But even with the new interviews, there was still a substantial impediment to the investigation—the many layers of suspicion that had been built up over the years among the different agencies. And, to Toensing's dismay, if there were any officials who were more distrusted than anyone else, it was those damn lawyers at the Justice Department. So she methodically set out to unravel the suspicion and build up the trust among the government agencies, a trust that would be vital if Rashid or Abu Ibrahim were ever to be apprehended. Ironically, it took a series of terrorist acts against the United States in 1985 to accomplish just that sort of interagency bonding.

On June 14, 1985, Toensing was driving to Boston's Logan Airport, having just attended her son's high school graduation in New Hampshire. About half an hour away from Boston, she heard a news bulletin on the radio that a TWA jet had been hijacked after it had taken off from Athens. Immediately she pulled over to a pay phone and called her deputy at the Justice Department, Lawrence Lippe. "Who's at the FBI command center?" she wanted to know.

"Why?" asked Lippe.

"Because there's been a hijacking!" she screamed back over the din of nearby traffic.

Toensing then instructed Lippe to dispatch lawyers to the FBI and CIA to make sure that all legal evidence could be preserved if prosecutions were warranted. But at the FBI, unaccustomed to Justice Department lawyers looking over its shoulder, there was resistance to any Justice attorney meddling. When Lippe went to the command center, FBI official Wayne Gilbert began screaming at him to leave, telling him that he could get involved *after* the event but that he was not welcome at the operations center. Clearly, the FBI was concerned about Justice compromising a source. The fibbies had been screwed before by Justice when attornies were allowed to sit in situation rooms monitoring crimes in progress. Lippe wouldn't take no for an answer and he was begrudgingly allowed to enter the command center.

Three months later, the potential for a flare-up between Justice and the FBI again materialized—during the hijacking of the *Achille Lauro*.

Toensing ordered her employees to be present at the agencies that were operationally in charge of the case. If a case was to be made against the terrorists, then a lawyer would have to advise on how best to preserve evidence. Again, the FBI accepted, though not too happily, the presence of the Justice Department lawyers.

Several weeks later, terrorists struck again, this time in Malta, when an Egyptair plane was hijacked. Toensing's attorneys immediately swung into action.

"By the time the Malta hijacking occurred, the FBI had the coffee already warm for us." And so by the end of 1985, Toensing, working together with her tireless attorneys, Lawrence Lippe and Karen Morrissette, had established a close working relationship with the FBI and CIA that would be critically important in developing an airtight case against Rashid. Toensing and other Justice Department officials credit Morrissette with keeping the case alive more than anyone else.

By 1986, the Rashid investigation kicked into high gear—but first the Justice Department and FBI got an opportunity to practice, in an operation involving another terrorist, Fawaz Younis.

Younis had hijacked a Royal Jordanian jet in June 1985 as it took off from Beirut. He later destroyed the aircraft but allowed the hostages to leave unharmed. Almost two years of planning went into Operation Goldenrod, involving officals from the CIA, Justice Department, FBI, National Security Council, and Drug Enforcement Agency. On September 12, 1987, after having been lured to international waters near Cyprus ostensibly to make a drug buy, Younis was apprehended by FBI agents posing as drug traffickers.

A former Lebanese Amal operative and onetime used-car dealer, Younis was not a particularly high-level terrorist—after all, no one was killed in his operation. Even FBI officials had a hard time remembering the specific act he had committed. Yet the fact remained that he became the first target of the bill that gave the FBI new extraterritorial jurisdiction to prosecute terrorists. The capture of Younis demonstrated that the Justice Department's new aggressive anti-terrorism mandate was indeed workable.

Prosecutors were also mindful of another factor: The five-year statute of limitations on an indictment against Rashid would expire in August 1988. "Because the clock was ticking," recalled Toensing, "it was necessary to begin the indictment process."

In Washington, Justice Department prosecutors set in motion the next-to-final legal stage of the operation to get Rashid: On January 15, 1987, a grand jury was sworn in at the United States District Court for the District of Columbia. Though all grand juries are secret, this one took place under extraordinarily heavy security. The case pitted the United States of America versus Mohammed Rashid, Abu Ibrahim, and Christine Pinter (a.k.a. Fatima Rashid).

Adnan was flown to Washington, escorted by several marshals. Security was very tight for him; the Justice Department and FBI did not want to take any chances.

It had been a little more than two years since Adnan had come to the United States.

In the closed courtroom, Adnan told his story step by step. He went over every detail in response to Dan Bent's patient questioning. It was tedious. "How did you come to Switzerland?" "What did you bring to Switzerland?" He had to repeat everything. His English was still not very good, so he was forced to rephrase his responses when his answers were not clear. Next to the witness stand, a large map had been propped up. Adnan pointed to the route he and his bomb had taken.

During a break in the testimony, a grand juror approached Bent and told him that she wanted Adnan to come live with her family, that he deserved to be part of an American citizen's home because of the tremendous sacrifice he had made. Bent told her it wasn't such a good idea, since she was supposed to be an impartial juror—but he would nonetheless pass the message along to Adnan.

Adnan testified for two days, which translated into more than two hundred pages of testimony. On his flight back home, he felt triumphant. Even though he was no longer in the Witness Protection Program, he had kept his promise to the United States. He felt good about being part of this strange process—the grand jury. He knew it was very important. But he thought that perhaps his testimony would be given to other parts of the government so they could read with their own eyes his testimony and see the evidence of Iraqi terrorism. What he didn't realize was that the government didn't work that way.

On July 14, 1987, the grand jury returned a sealed multiple indictment against Rashid, Ibrahim, and Pinter. The indictment charged that the "May 15 Organization was a terrorist group whose objective was to promote the Palestinian cause by coercing and intimidating by means of force and violence, causing personal injury to civilians, and causing economic damage to American and Israeli interests around the world." The defendants were charged with nine counts, including conspiracy to destroy two American aircraft, conspiracy to commit murder, murder, aircraft sabotage, and placing bombs aboard aircraft.

Once the indictments were issued, the burden shifted to the intelligence community to keep track of the movements of the indicted three. Abu Ibrahim didn't move out of Baghdad, it seemed. But Rashid and his wife had been seen in various countries in Europe, the Middle East, and Asia. Intelligence reports showed that the couple was constantly moving about—Rashid more than his wife.

But a decision to have Rashid arrested had to take other factors into consideration beyond the fact that he was "gettable." Toensing recalled the dilemma she and others faced when seeing the reports on Rashid.

"It would be so maddening to know that he was traveling around under indictment and that for a while our hands were tied. We had to be very disciplined in finally deciding how we would get him. Because even though the president has the constitutional power to send agents to another country and arrest them when there is a valid arrest warrant, certainly there are foreign-policy considerations why the president would not do that very often."

Rashid, for example, routinely visited Tunisia. But U.S. officials realized that asking the Tunisian government to detain and extradite Rashid would put the Tunisians in a politically impossible situation. Home to the PLO, Tunisia could never cooperate in an operation against a Palestinian—even if it were done covertly. Arresting Rashid secretly and then spiriting him out of Tunisia was also given serious consideration—but then ruled out.

By late 1987, the CIA had learned that Rashid stayed for long periods of time in Khartoum with his wife and child. Again, officials considered an operation to snatch Rashid, but consideration of Sudanese political sensitivities, coupled with objections voiced by the Joint Chiefs of Staff, stopped any action. And Iraq, of course, the headquarters for Rashid and the terrorist chieftain Abu Ibrahim, was off limits.

Then, finally, the countdown began. The CIA's informant notified his handler that Rashid was planning to travel to other countries in April or May 1988. To which countries he wasn't sure, but it appeared that Yugoslavia and Greece would be on his intinerary. Greece would have to be the farthest west he would be going. It would be politically impossible to pull off an operation in any of the other countries he was visiting. From what the informant had said, intelligence officials concluded that Rashid was on a surveillance mission for future terrorist attacks.

One day during the last week of May, at an interagency anti-terrorism meeting in downtown Washington, FBI and Justice Department officials were told that Rashid would be arriving in Greece within the next forty-eight to seventy-two hours.

"We made the decision to go for it," recalled one of the participants.

13

The Capture

The tall, immaculately dressed man arrived at the Athens airport on May 30, 1988, on a flight from Yugoslavia. He went through Greek immigration, where he was asked to show his passport. Saying he was on his way to other countries and was making only a short stop in Greece, the man took out his Syrian passport and handed it over to the Greek officer. The officer studied it for a minute, then ran the number through the master computer containing suspicious passport numbers. Sure enough, the number came up on the list. The man was asked to step aside and enter a small room, where he was told that he was being detained.

Several days before, the United States requested that Interpol provide the Greek government with several Middle East passport numbers that were known to be false. Interpol didn't explain, but asked Greece to detain anyone who was using any of those passports. Greece, which was a member of Interpol, readily agreed.

When the Greeks found they had detained one of the holders of the passports in question, they informed Interpol, which in turn informed the American embassy in Athens. " 'We got this guy that you asked for—now what do you want us to do with him?' was the essence of the message," recalled a diplomat serving at the embassy at the time. Now the United States was ready to enter the picture.

"We told the Greeks who he was," recalled a Justice Department official, "and they said, 'Oh shit!' " When Greek officials demanded proof, the Americans were ready, having prepared extensive documents and files. Justice Department officials then began turning over reams of evidence to Greek prosecutors, including a Greek translation of the sealed indictment. The material had been specifically prepared to meet the legal requirements of Greek juridical standards.

But the man arrested by the Greek government insisted that he was not Mohammed Rashid. He said his name, as written on his passport, was Mohammed Hamdan, that he was thirty-four, and that he was a Syrian citizen. He said the arrest was a case of mistaken identity and he demanded to be freed. The Greek government said nothing.

Seventy-two hours after Rashid had been detained, the United States formally asked Greece to extradite Rashid to the United States. Justice Department lawyers filed a brief with the Greek government, pointing out that under the terms of the 1971 Montreal Convention, signed by members of the Civil Aviation Organization, which included the United States and Greece, anyone charged with acts of terrorism against airliners must be handed over to the country that has charged them or be put on trial by the country holding them. Included in the request was indisputable proof that the man traveling on the Syrian passport was indeed Mohammed Rashid, a man wanted in connection with the 1982 bombing of a Pan Am plane.

The U.S. request for extradition was made by a senior American diplomat in a meeting with Prime Minister Andreas Papandreou. But at the meeting, Papandreou did not commit himself one way or another, saying that it was a matter for the Greek courts to decide. In fact, the ultimate authority for extraditing Rashid rested with the prime minister. The American diplomat had an uneasy feeling in his stomach as he left the meeting. "We knew that Greece would scream and holler, but we felt that if we kicked it up to the level of bilateral American-Greek relations, Papandreou would acquiesce. When I walked out of that meeting, I knew that we had given those bastards more credit than we should have."

Three days later, Greece formally refused the American request, saying that the evidence provided by the United States was not sufficient to justify extradition. Besides, Greek officials said, an extradition request would have to wind itself through the Greek courts, a process, a spokesman hastened to add, that could take "years."

From the very beginning, officials at the Justice Department had had serious qualms about relying on the Greek government to arrest Rashid. Greece had already proved to have an abysmal record on prosecuting terrorists, particularly Palestinian terrorists. In 1984, the Greeks had released Fouad Hussein Shara, even though they had incontestable proof that he was involved in the conspiracy to blow up the El Al airliner. In 1987, the United States accused Greece of negotiating a "sweetheart" deal with the notorious Abu Nidal organization, in which Nidal was permitted to operate a front company in Athens that posed as an export-import firm but in fact was a logistics office for Nidal's operations. The export-import company was finally shut down as a result of American pressure, but Papandreou bitterly attacked the United States for making the accusation and trying to besmirch Greece's reputation.

Greece's record with home-grown terrorists was not that much better. They apparently had free reign in Greece, having assassinated several American officials during the previous decade. The CIA station chief in Athens, Richard Welch, was shot to death in 1975 by a group calling itself November 17—named after a November 17, 1973, student uprising against the Greek military junta. Then, in 1983, U.S. Navy captain George Tsantes was executed as he drove to work. His chauffeur was also slain. Since its inception in 1973, no member of the November 17 organization had ever been caught by authorities.

Among large segments of the Greek population there was a visceral anti-American mood, and this was especially true for followers of the ruling Panhellenic Socialist Movement. Some leading members of the party had actually trained in PLO camps. Sifis Valyrakis, the deputy minister of public order, for example, was schooled in terrorist warfare in southern Lebanon by PLO fighters in the early 1970s. There was a feeling in certain quarters of the CIA that Greece had swung so far to the left that it had become thoroughly compromised by Soviet intelligence as well.

As the United States waited to see what the Greek government would do about Rashid, American diplomats kept up the pressure. L. Paul Bremer from the State Department's Office for Combatting Terrorism was dispatched to Athens to meet with Greek leaders. He and other U.S. officials let it be known that they viewed the

Rashid matter as one of the most important tests of Greek-U.S. bilateral relations. Publicly, the United States said nothing, although reports began leaking out in the Greek press that the United States had demanded the extradition of Rashid. The State Department and White House refused to comment.

In the meantime, according to officials stationed in the American embassy in Athens, the PLO explicitly warned the Greek government against extraditing Rashid to the United States. On June 12, a senior official of the Greek Ministry of Public Order told the press in Athens that Greece would put Rashid on trial for traveling on a false passport. It was a holding action, designed to postpone the more serious question of extradition.

In late June, Rashid was put on trial in a Greek courtroom. There was extraordinary security—Greek sharpshooters on nearby rooftops, heavily armed Greek police and security men throughout the courthouse. During the trial, Rashid boldly declared that he was a member of the Palestine Liberation Organization but continued to insist that he was not Mohammed Rashid. In perfect English, he asserted, "I am a member of the PLO and the Palestine Liberation Army." He contended, however, that it was his first time ever in Greece, and asserted that because he was a Palestinian, he was unable to obtain a bona fide passport; "Palestinians," he said, "have no country."

For the trial, the PLO diplomatic mission in Athens provided a Greek-Arabic interpreter, hired a Greek attorney to provide Rashid with legal counsel, and sent a high-ranking PLO official to attend the proceedings daily.

A Greek police official testified that Rashid's fingerprints were the same as those of a person who had served a prison sentence in Greece from 1973 through 1976 for possession of drugs. And that person, according to Greek records, was positively identified at the time as Mohammed Rashid. The police expert argued convincingly that the defendant was Mohammed Rashid and *not* Mohammed Hamdan.

As the trial unfolded, a bloody terrorist attack, something the Greeks had desperately feared, occurred on Greek soil. A gunman attacked the ferryboat *City of Poros* in Piraeus harbor on July 13. Hand grenades were thrown and machine-gun fire was sprayed at the hundreds of foreign tourists on board, who dropped like paper targets. Nine people died and more than ninety-eight were wounded. Initially, Greek police believed the attack to have been an effort to force the release of Rashid. Later they discovered that it had been organized by Abu Nidal, a bitter foe of Yasser Arafat, prompting reporters to allege there was no connection between the attack and Rashid's trial. To this day, intelligence agencies are unsure whether the attack was related to Rashid.

On July 15, before a packed crowd in the hot and humid courtroom, the three judges announced their verdict: Rashid was guilty of entering Greece with a false Syrian passport and was sentenced to seven months in jail.

In Washington, State Department spokeswoman Phyllis Oakley publicly requested that Greece initiate extradition hearings to facilitate a U.S. trial of Rashid. Greek law required that Rashid serve out his sentence, but that he could be extradited upon its completion. Privately, American counterterrorist officials expressed deep frustration with Greece and fears that Rashid would be allowed to get off once his term was finished.

In the meantime, the Athens Appeals Council, the

Greek equivalent of an American grand jury, began hearing secret testimony from American officials on the case against Rashid. The evidence included both the 1982 bombing of the Pan Am plane that killed fourteen-year-old Toru Ozawa and the 1986 bombing of the TWA plane over Greece that killed four Americans. On August 3, the council said that it would make a determination within two days on whether Greece would allow the extradition of Rashid. But two days later, it announced it was postponing its decision until September.

In response to reports that the PLO had pressured the Greek government, a State Department spokesman issued an unusually strong statement: "If the report is true on this request not to extradite, the PLO's attempt to influence the legal proceedings between the government in Greece and the United States would raise serious questions about the attitudes of the PLO toward the scourge of international terrorism. We would find reprehensible any attempt by the PLO to protect a known terrorist. The PLO should repudiate this stance."

For the State Department, it was particularly vital that the PLO comply. Already, secret negotiations had begun to arrive at a formula by which the United States could recognize the PLO, and it required the PLO's unconditional reununciation of terror. If the PLO adopted such a public stance in support of a known terrorist, it would surely jeopardize the administration's plans for a direct dialogue with them.

Meanwhile, the Athens Appeals Council met behind closed doors to hear testimony of a parade of witnesses and examine supporting documents. On September 5, the council announced that it had postponed once again a final decision on whether Rashid should be extradited. It was clear that Greece wanted the problem to go away—but it was just as clear that it wouldn't. And the Americans kept up the pressure—but so did the PLO, regardless of the U.S. warnings. The PLO diplomatic mission in Athens privately warned the Greek government of unknown "consequences" if Rashid were extradited.

On October 10, the council finally issued a long-awaited decision: It recommended by a vote of 2–1 that Rashid be extradited to the United States. A stunning upset to the Palestine Liberation Organization, the ruling drew a warm congratulatory response from the United States. But the saga of Rashid was far from over. His PLO-paid lawyers filed an appeal with the Greek Supreme Court. Then they did something else. A PLO front organization issued a blatant threat against the Greek government if Rashid were not immediately freed.

As the Greek Supreme Court wrestled with the case, the true colors of the Greek-ruled Panhellenic Socialist Movement began to show. Another extradition case had been before the Greek government. In 1984 the Supreme Court had agreed to extradite a Palestinian terrorist, Abdel Osama Zomar, to Italy for his involvement in the brutal attack on Rome's main synagogue in September 1982. The attack had left a two-year-old boy dead and wounded thirty-seven worshipers. Zomar was apprehended two months later on the Greek-Turkish border, when police inspected his car and found it full of explosives. There was such a large amount of explosives in his car's paneling that the Greek police called it a bomb on wheels. The evidence presented by Italian prosecutors of Zomar's participation in the attack was overwhelming. Yet the Greek government had put the extradition agreement on hold.

In December 1988, the Greek justice minister finally issued his decision in the Zomar case. Ruling that the terrorist "was acting in the struggle for the reacquisition of his homeland," Justice Minister Vassilis Rotis nullified the extradition agreement and ordered Zomar freed from jail and put on the Olympic Airways plane of his choice to any country in the world. Not surprisingly, Zomar chose Libya. As one Justice Department official bitterly dubbed the act, "This was the Greek government's frequent-flyer program."

The outcry from the United States was swift and biting. An administration official leaked a report that the White House was considering slapping a terrorist advisory alert on Greece—thereby effectively stopping American tourism there. The last time that was done was in 1985—which Greek tourist officials estimated cost the Greeks some $100 million in lost revenues.

The U.S. attorney general, Dick Thornburgh, happened to be in Greece when the Zomar decision was made. Thornburgh met with Minister Rotis, calling the decision "deplorable." An editorial in *The Washington Post* condemned the Greek government for its "shameful decision," and warned that "if such a travesty occurs in the case of Mohammed Rashid, Americans will be outraged." And then, taking a cue from the administration, the editorial said that if "Athens continues to obstruct the efforts of civilized nations to protect international air travel and punish terrorists, there must be sanctions."

In the U.S. House of Representatives, a resolution was introduced calling on Greece to allow extradition of Rashid. On February 14, 1990, ten U.S. senators sent a letter to the Greek prime minister. "We are writing to strongly urge you to extradite Mohammed Rashid to the United

States," the letter said, going on to warn that a decision not to allow the extradition would "weigh heavily on the U.S. Senate's future assessment of U.S.-Greek relations." The following week, Secretary of State James Baker discussed the Rashid case when he met with Prime Minister Papandreou in Athens. According to State Department officials, Secretary Baker let the prime minister know that the United States viewed Rashid's extradition as a "test of Greek-U.S. relations."

Greece's supersensitivity to the case was demonstrated by the way it handled a minor incident involving Rashid. On February 17, his prison cell in the Korydallos jail was searched as part of a random inspection, and guards found two makeshift stilettos. Rashid was immediately charged with possessing illegal weapons, and a three-member court of appeals began to consider the case. On February 20, the court heard testimony from Rashid, who admitted possession of the knives but said he needed them "because I fear for my life [and] I also fear they may extradite me to the United States." As the court readied its verdict later that afternoon, a bomb threat emptied the courthouse. Bomb-squad units with bomb-sniffing dogs arrived, but found nothing. When the judges returned, they announced that they had found Rashid not guilty.

The Piraeus district attorney immediately challenged the ruling, forcing Rashid's retrial. A month later, Rashid was found guilty and sentenced to eight additional months in jail, although, in an unusual twist, the court gave Rashid the opportunity to pay a fine of 96,000 drachma—equivalent at the time to $620—instead of serving his sentence. Rashid's lawyer announced to the press that he didn't know what his client would do. "We don't know what the PLO wants. They may want to pay the fine or they may want him to serve it out." Because Rashid had completed his first sentence—for having a false passport—the new sentence was critical in ensuring that Rashid did not leave Greece a free man.

The debate over Rashid continued. For the Greek government, it was a political hot potato the temperature of which had been raised to radioactive levels. Two senior magistrates were murdered in a spate of attacks that created a climate of fear within the country's judicial branch. In early March, terrorists attacked the home of a senior appeals judge—a warning not to allow Rashid's extradition. Though the damage was slight—a bomb blast blew out the door to the judge's apartment—the message was not lost. On March 15, the Greek Supreme Court, which had been scheduled to rule on Rashid's appeal, announced that it had again postponed—it was the third time—a hearing on Rashid's extradition. Ten minutes into it, one of the five justices had become "ill." The president of the court, Vassilis Lambides, then announced that "one member of the court has just told us that he suddenly feels unwell and because of this I recommend a postponement." Courtroom spectators, composed largely of Rashid sympathizers, erupted into shouts of "Hands off the PLO!" This was the sixth Greek Supreme Court justice to have resigned or withdrawn on account of illness over the preceding four months of deliberations.

The security under which the Supreme Court met was extraordinary and unprecedented for Greece. More than one thousand policemen guarded the imposing marble building. Police snipers were clearly visible on nearby rooftops.

Several days later, the Supreme Court resumed its behind-the-scenes deliberations. But the Greek track record did not leave U.S. officials hopeful. Victoria Toensing recalled, "We always feared that the Greek government would sort of slip him out under guard at night, through their borders, and give him a free trip back to some other Middle East country. They had done it just a few months before, with [Zomar]."

On May 13, the court announced that it had reached a verdict. The courtroom was overflowing with Greek security people and spectators. Court photographers were instructed to leave as the justices convened to issue their decision. As silence hung in the air, the head of the court announced that the Greek Supreme Court had decided to uphold the extradition of Rashid to the United States.

The decision was immediately applauded by U.S. Attorney General Thornburgh. "The court's decision sends a strong signal around the world that outright, senseless murder cannot be excused under the dubious claim of political motivation. There's nothing political about blowing up innocent civilians in the sky." The final decision regarding Rashid's extradition was now in the hands of the Greek government; even though the court had made its decision, the justice minister had the power to authorize that the decision be implemented—or *not* be implemented. And in political reality, the decision ultimately rested with the Greek prime minister.

At the Justice Department in Washington, attorneys working on the case waited anxiously for Papandreou to make a ruling—hoping that, despite his government's record, he would affirm the court's ruling. But no one was holding his or her breath. Recalled Toensing, "Even though the Greek Supreme Court had ruled in favor and even though we had applied as much pressure as we could, we were essentially dealing with a government that did not want to uphold international law."

So it was not entirely unexpected when Toensing and others at the Justice Department learned on May 16 of the decision made that morning by the Papandreou government: An official Greek spokesman said the decision on Rashid's extradition had been "postponed" until after the Greek elections, which were scheduled for June. The United States said nothing, but privately officials fumed. The American embassy in Athens was instructed to strongly protest Greece's decision. A demarche was delivered to the Greek Foreign Ministry on May 30.

In the June elections, the eight-year-old Papandreou government was soundly defeated. On July 25, the new government, a conservative-communist coalition consisting of the New Democracy party and the Communist party, announced that a decision on Rashid's extradition was again being put off until general elections were held in the fall. He would be kept in jail pending the decision. The interim government was split along ideological lines. In interviews with Greek newspapers, Constantine Mitsotakis said he was inclined to allow the extradition of Rashid to the United States. But his partner, Interior Minister Nikos Kostantopoulous, said he was against it. Kostantopoulous was not exactly a disinterested party: Before the election, he had served as an attorney for Rashid. Essentially the government was paralyzed—and prevented from doing anything.

In the fall election, a new coalition assumed power, but once again, an internal split prevented the government from making any decision. It was the third such Greek government that had postponed a decision on the volatile Rashid extradition issue.

The Rashid case sat in the lap of the Greek government over the next twelve months. There was no movement one way or another. The only movement occurred in March 1990, when the justice minister, Constantine Stamatis, announced that Rashid "might" be tried in Greece for the 1982 bombing of Pan Am Flight 830, and therefore would not be extradited to the United States. Because the justice minister's announcement was couched in uncertainty, its purpose, Greek policy analysts later said, was to serve as a trial balloon.

A flurry of diplomatic exchanges between Washington and Athens followed, with Washington requesting "clarification" from the Greek government. But if there was one thing the Greek regime could not deliver, it was "clarification" of the Rashid issue. A major internal debate had broken out among the differing factions of the Greek government. Officially the issue was still stuck in dead center, caught between those who wanted to set the Palestinian free and those sympathetic to the U.S. request.

Privately, U.S. officials began arduous negotiations over the disposition of Rashid's status, raising for the first time the possibility that Washington might accept a compromise in which Rashid would be tried in Greece. That could only happen if the Greek government evinced a sincere and genuine desire to apply justice. The new Greek government, under the leadership of Miksotakis, was considered a friend of the United States. Through the summer, a series of meetings were held in both Washington and Athens—although Washington still insisted officially on extradition.

* * *

In September 1990, Greek prosecutors began making unannounced visits to Rashid in his cell in Korydallos prison. There, Rashid was asked a series of questions regarding the 1982 Pan Am bombing. It was now clear that the Greek government had made up its mind.

On September 18, a special Greek judicial team, headed by a magistrate, visited the terrorist. The magistrate did not come to ask him any questions. Rashid was asked to stand as the magistrate informed him that he had been indicted for his involvement in the 1982 bombing. In the meeting, which lasted about an hour, the magistrate read to Rashid the four charges for which he would be tried: homicide, seizure of an aircraft, placement of explosive devices in an aircraft, and damage to an aircraft.

The next day, the Greek Justice Ministry announced that Rashid would be tried in Greece and would not be extradited to the United States. But as far as the United States Justice Department was concerned, at least the Greek government had finally demonstrated that it was serious about prosecuting the terrorist. After more than two years of wrangling, the issue was decided. It was not the best solution, but it was one the United States could live with.

14

The United States Turns
a Blind Eye

The news that Rashid had been caught came as a shock
to Adnan. He had not expected that the United States
would ever be able to find his ex-friend, the master of
deception. He listened in amazement as the Justice Department official told him that Rashid was now in a prison
in Greece—and that the United States would try to extradite him. But as the legal drama surrounding Rashid
started stretching out, Adnan was kept on the back
burner, not told of any other developments.

Adnan was now back in the Witness Protection Program—he had agreed to rejoin in late 1987. His Justice
Department handlers promised him a passport—after he
had pleaded for one for years. Without a passport he was
no one—just like his earlier days in Syria. A passport
would have provided the most tangible evidence yet that
the United States fully accepted him as a citizen. He
dreamed he would carry it around with him at all times.
He dreamed that when he traveled abroad, he would simply flash it to foreign immigration officials—and they
would genuflect and welcome him. Of course, in reality,

that would never happen—but his dreams indicated how important acquiring a passport had become to him.

The Witness Protection Program forced him to relocate again—this time to a midwestern city. It was cold, bitterly cold. And incredibly windy. He had never experienced a temperature of minus 50 degrees before. He was amazed that humans could live in such a climate.

Within a month, he had asked the marshals to relocate him again. This time, it was to a southern state. And though the warmer climate was much more hospitable, it was there that Adnan was reminded of a nagging problem he had faced the previous time he was in the program. An unsavory fact was that many of the people being protected either had criminal backgrounds or exploited their new identities to avoid paying debts. As a result, many of those in the program were looked upon with great suspicion by the very marshals who were responsible for protecting their lives.

Adnan felt that he, too, was looked upon with suspicion—that the marshals acted as if they were doing him a favor rather than the other way around. Adnan was not a witness who had entered the program because of a plea bargain, as many had done—buying their freedom by testifying against someone else. He had come to the United States of his own free volition. He was not a criminal or a low-life, yet he felt that the marshals in this southern state treated him with the same contempt with which they viewed hardened and unrepentant criminals.

Adnan became increasingly depressed about his bleak situation. He was estranged from nearly everything in the world. And he still didn't have a passport—though it had been promised him for nearly two years. He began thinking about suicide.

Adnan reckoned that the easiest way would be a car accident. He habitually exceeded the speed limit, hoping that he'd increase his chances of dying. He became paranoid, believing that the United States would kill him as soon as it got what it wanted from him. After all, he was nothing but a pain in the ass—complaining all the time. They were surely sick of him, he thought.

Then, in the fall of 1990, he heard from the Justice Department. Rashid was going to be tried in Greece. As a result, Adnan would have to come to Washington. Suddenly, he felt better about himself. He didn't know exactly why. Perhaps it was because he was being wooed by the Justice Department again. They told him how important his testimony would be. He became manic, his emotions ranging from deep despair to exuberance. In a strange way, his sense of esteem seemed to have become fused to the case against Rashid.

For Adnan it was a momentous trip going back to Washington. As his security required, he could not fly directly, so he first flew to another city, changed planes, and then flew to Washington. At National Airport, he was greeted by five armed federal marshals and whisked away in a two-car convoy to a hotel in downtown Washington, where the marshals had registered him under yet another alias. In charge of the marshal security detail was an older woman—Adnan estimated she was in her sixties—who ensured that the hotel and traffic routes were secure. She carried a pistol in a shoulder holster under her jacket and barked out commands sternly and with authority—so much so that she reminded Adnan of Colonel Majoub from his days in the Palestine Liberation Army. Except she was in better shape than the fat colonel.

This was the first time in three years that Adnan had been flown to Washington by the Justice Department. He was to give six hours of secret testimony over a two-day period to U.S. prosecutors and visiting Greek judicial investigators.

Adnan was told by his Justice Department handler that even though he had given the same testimony before, they had to prove to the Greeks that the United States indeed had a reliable secret witness. His testimony was desperately needed by the Greek prosecutors to prepare for this long-awaited case.

After testifying, Adnan returned home. He felt good about himself. Things had gone well, he was told. He would be the key witness in the trial against Rashid. He felt he was making a contribution to the United States. Justice Department officials still didn't know when the trial would take place, but it seemed imminent.

A week later, Adnan received a phone call from *Time* magazine reporter Jay Peterzell notifying him that his name had just leaked out in the Greek press as the secret American witness against Rashid. The article said Adnan had been living in the United States since 1984.

Adnan immediately called Allen Maxell, one of his FBI handlers, to complain. "My real name is in the Greek newspapers! You told me that would not happen!"

Maxwell refused to believe it. "That's impossible," he insisted. Later that day, Adnan faxed Maxwell a copy of the Greek newspaper that had indeed cited his name.

Maxwell called back, very apologetic, saying that the United States had no idea that this would happen, and the government did not have any control over information once the Greeks got a hold of it. Maxwell said he was very sorry for what had happened. Adnan was crushed by this breach of security—it wasn't so much the increased threat to himself that worried him, but the danger posed to his family still living in Baghdad.

Throughout his six years in the United States, Adnan found that he could occasionally call his family in Baghdad—his two sisters, a brother, and dozens of nieces, nephews, and cousins. He was always careful not to say anything sensitive over the telephone. He was told by American intelligence officials that Iraqi authorities were listening to these conversations—and that they apparently permitted the telephone calls in the hope Adnan would reveal something compromising. If he revealed any information deemed to be important by Iraq, he could put his family in great danger. As much as Adnan wanted to tell his brother Jamal, whom he was very close to, what he had been doing—he couldn't. He always used to share moments of joy and happiness with Jamal, such moments as meeting a beautiful woman or buying a new car.

Adnan had to be careful even in his letters, which had to be routed through other countries. He could not reveal anything that might give away his whereabouts, which meant that the letters were usually very short. Painfully short. He always wanted to tell his brother more—but he couldn't.

When he came to the United States, the FBI and Justice Department promised him total anonymity, as much for his sake as for his family's.

It was this threat that had bothered him the most about defecting. He loved his family. Because he had never married or had children, he had become very attached to his sisters and brother—and was almost a surrogate father to his nieces and nephews. Adnan missed seeing them more than anything in the world. "If I could have one wish granted," he said, "it would be to see my family." Leaving them behind in 1982 was painful—and the pain was compounded when it appeared that the Iraqi government would retaliate against his family.

For whatever reasons, the Iraqi government did not imprison Adnan's family, though they were always under surveillance and their passports had been lifted. His brother's cars were confiscated. And on one occasion, Abu Ibrahim had made a menacing visit. But members of his family were still able to hold on to decently paying jobs. Considering what the Iraqi Mukhabarat *could* have done, Adnan felt that they remained relatively unscathed.

Why the Iraqi government didn't immediately retaliate against his family, Adnan could never figure out. But whatever the reason, their welfare and safety always weighed on his mind, the only piece of unfinished business with which his conscience had continued to wrestle. When the Greek newspaper printed his name, it revealed for the first time to the outside world the fact that he had secretly defected to the United States in 1984 and that he was going to be the principal witness against Mohammed Rashid.

While the Iraqis and Abu Ibrahim clearly knew that Adnan had disappeared, they could not have known too much more than that with any certainty. Adnan had been advised by American intelligence agents that he should assume that Ibrahim and the rest "suspected" that he had defected. After all, the Americans had received a raw intelligence report two years before that Iraq had offered a bounty to anyone who would kill Adnan.

Beyond intuition and suspicion, Ibrahim and his Iraqi benefactors had had no way of knowing what had really happened to Adnan. The article in the Greek newspaper

destroyed eight years of carefully nurtured anonymity and
secrecy. It was all over. Adnan waited with a sense of
foreboding.

A week after discovering that his story was now public in
Europe, Adnan spoke to his brother Jamal in Baghdad.
Jamal was uncharacteristically terse. Then he told Adnan,
"Your name was just printed in a Baghdad newspaper—
and everything else was told, too."

In the eight years since he had made that fateful decision to defect, this was the worst moment Adnan had
experienced. He was sick, sick to his stomach. He quickly
recovered his composure, knowing that he could not afford to let the Mukhabarat listening in know how concerned he was about his family. He wanted to keep the
telephone line to his brother permanently intact, like an
international intercom. Adnan kept prolonging the conversation, but his brother was getting very uncomfortable.
He had to go, he told Adnan. God be with you, he blessed
him in Arabic.

When he hung up the telephone, Adnan sat in his
kitchen and stared out the window. He was stricken with
fear about what would happen next. He called the FBI
again. "You promised this would not happen," he cried.
But there was nothing further that could be done, nothing
to put the genie back in the bottle. The old feelings of
despair returned. Overcome with horrible thoughts about
what would happen to his family, he felt immensely guilty,
regretting everything he had done since his flight to Geneva in 1982.

Since that time, Adnan has tried repeatedly to communicate again with Jamal. He has tried frequently through
the international operator but the calls will not go

through. Again and again, he has tried dialing—and each time, the operator says that the connection will not go through. Why, he asks the operator, hoping that perhaps she will tell him whether his brother's telephone is working or not. But there is nothing more she ever tells him.

His father still lived in Damascus, Adnan knew. He hadn't spoken to him in some time, but after his last conversation with Jamal, he called his father's home. Abu Adnan answered the phone. "He began crying and crying," Adnan recalled. "He told me he was so happy to hear my voice."

Soon a letter arrived from his youngest sister, who also lived in Damascus. She wrote to say that she was married and had children. Adnan reminisced about the day he last saw her, more than twelve years before—she was a girl of ten. Now she was a full-grown woman and mother. Missing those years hurt. He had vanished from her life. How does a child make sense of a stolen heart? She never tried. Her note was addressed to "The One Who Forgot His Sister."

Adnan thought a lot about what had happened to him over the previous eight years. It seemed as if his odyssey were about to reach a climax. The Justice Department notified him that the trial against Rashid might start as soon as January 1991. Since his name was already public knowledge, there was no sense trying to remain a classified witness. Would he agree to go to Greece to testify in an open courtroom? Yes, he said, he would. There would be an increased threat to his life—there was no denying that, they told him. Rashid and his benefactors, Abu Ibrahim and the PLO, would surely attempt to have him killed.

But the Justice Department officials would travel with him and stay with him at all times.

Strangely, Adnan bore no ill will toward Mohammed Rashid. He even felt sorry for him. "He's very gentle and he listens five times more than he speaks," Adnan said. "You feel like he's distracted all the time. I believe he's scared." Kind words for a man who would probably kill him in a second, a man who no doubt would try to inflict revenge on his family. Adnan may very well have been describing himself when he spoke of Rashid. Adnan, too, seems distracted most of the time now. He's scared, a man who has been living the life of someone constantly on the run, always looking over his shoulder. He seems like a prisoner of sorts, imprisoned by fear of the unknown.

Thousands of miles away, across an ocean, his former friend Mohammed Rashid, locked up in a maximum-security cell at the Korydallos prison, is, in a sense, freer than Adnan. Despite his incarceration and the fact that he has been charged with homicide, he carries himself with an air of supreme self-confidence. When he shows up in court surrounded by a phalanx of policemen, a motley group of people—punks, young men and women in black leather, well-known leftists, and student activists—consistently turn up to support him, often grabbing the best seats in the courtroom.

Rashid never stoops and rarely shows any sign of emotion, remaining soft-spoken and mild-mannered. He is an immaculate dresser—all his financial needs are taken care of by the PLO—and appears to take great pride in his appearance; he is always well groomed and never unshaven. If there is any facial expression, it usually leads to the most radiant of smiles—this from a man who tried to blow up at least ten airplanes, a man who would use his child as cover for him as he placed deadly bombs underneath airplane seats. No doubt, when Rashid gets out of prison he will have a stamped passport waiting for him—which is a lot more than Adnan Awad has in the United States.

15

The Iraqi Terror Network

That Adnan had been brought to the United States in 1984 and had come to Washington only three times was, in and of itself, a damning indictment of American policy. The tragedy is that instead of being sequestered by the government, essentially ignored except for specific testimony for a trial that would take place far from American soil, Adnan Awad could have provided the spark that might have induced policymakers to rethink their tilt toward Iraq, a tilt that snowballed into a colossal mistake and eventually led to the Persian Gulf war. Even though, in the overall scheme of things, Adnan was not the biggest terrorist who ever stalked the earth—he was basically a courier—he was the only living cog in the terror machinery who could and would detail exactly how the machine was working. Back in 1982, when Iraq had just been taken off the list of nations supporting terrorism, Adnan could have provided eloquent testimony that Iraq was indeed controlled by a regime that was without question as abominable as its enemy Iran. But the United States had made a decision that it loathed and feared Iran—and, as a result, it embraced Iraq.

By the time Adnan testified in Washington in October 1990, Iraq had established one of the most elaborate and institutionalized terrorism networks in the entire world. Terrorism—practiced against Americans, Israelis, Kurds, Iraqi dissidents, and fellow Arabs—had become a rudimentary and extremely effective instrument of Iraqi foreign and domestic policy.

In its embassies in Europe, Iraq had put in place military intelligence attachés who served as terrorist liaisons, ordering surveillance on dissidents and Western targets, passing along money and instructions to terrorist operatives, smuggling weapons and explosives to terrorists, and recruiting and cultivating cells of Iraqi terrorists to serve as "sleepers"—operatives who could be activated *anytime* in the future. Iraq has consistently used its diplomatic pouch to transfer explosives and weapons to operatives in Asia and Europe.

In recent years, Western intelligence officials have pinpointed several Iraqi embassies known to have hosted specific Iraqi military intelligence officers whose sole mission was to serve as liaisons with terrorist groups and operatives. By 1989, surveillance by counterintelligence and counterterrorist agencies of several countries produced irrefutable evidence that these officers had routinely collected intelligence on Iraqi nationals, Israeli institutions, prominent Jewish citizens around the world, and Syrian and Iranian diplomats. The Iraqi embassies identified by the Western intelligence agencies as being most heavily involved in directing or collecting terrorist surveillance included those in Switzerland, Thailand, the Philippines, Great Britain, Norway, Greece, Italy, and the Netherlands.

Iraq also established international organizations, such as the National Union of Iraqi Students and the Iraqi National Student Association, that were nothing more than front groups designed to provide cover and legitimacy to Iraqi agents who spied on fellow countrymen and carried out occasional transfers of weapons. The organizations were funded directly out of Iraqi embassy slush funds in Asia and the Middle East.

In Lebanon, Sudan, Syria, Egypt, and Jordan, Iraqi military-intelligence officers coordinated attacks on Iraqi dissidents, Kurds, and Syrians. On January 18, 1988, for example, an Iraqi dissident was shot to death at a political convention in Khartoum. In Lebanon, intelligence officials say that more than fifty Iraqi dissidents were killed by Iraqi agents over the past decade.

Egyptian intelligence discovered in 1988 that the Iraqi embassy in Egypt had instructed Iraqi hit men to assassinate Iraqis and other Arabs who had become political opponents of Saddam Hussein. Egypt never made this information public, nor did it deport the Iraqi military attaché who had been the key official behind the plan. This was partly due to the extraordinarily close military collaboration between Egypt and Iraq at the time: Financed by Iraq, Egypt was secretly working on Project Condor 2, the development of a ballistic missile capable of carrying a nuclear warhead; Egypt acquired equipment and technology on Iraq's behalf from international consortiums and foreign countries such as Brazil.

In Europe, American and British intelligence officials say that since 1982 Iraqi agents have assassinated at least a dozen Iraqi exiles in Sweden, France, Belgium, Norway,

Turkey, Greece, and Great Britain. In the United States, according to an internal 1990 FBI report, at least four Iraqis and other Arabs have died under "mysterious and unnatural circumstances." The slain men were either exiled Iraqi dissidents or enemies of the Iraqi Baath party.

One of the most vicious arms of the Iraqi government used to carry out terror attacks has been the Baath party security apparatus. The original Baath party was founded by Michel Aflaq, a Syrian Christian who championed Arab unity. For years, he was the nominal head of the Iraqi and Syrian Baath party. But in the sixties, a split developed in the two regional branches in Damascus and Baghdad.

When the Iraqi Baath party assumed control of the Iraqi government in 1968, its rival Syrian branch became nervous and was antagonistic toward the newly proclaimed Iraqi nationalism. In Iraq, the Baath party emerged as a small conspiratorial group whose membership was tightly controlled and restricted. By 1975, there were only ten thousand members. But when Saddam Hussein took over Iraq in 1979, he expanded it dramatically—requiring all military officers to join. It became his equivalent of the Communist party.

In the meantime, the Baath party developed its very own intelligence and security apparatus that worked out of Iraqi embassies.

In the United States, Iraqi dissidents have been targeted for execution by assassins dispatched through the Iraqi embassy in New York and by the Iraqi United Nations mission, also in New York. In January 1990, for example, an Iraqi diplomat tried to arrange the executions of two Iraqi dissident leaders living in the States. FBI agents had wiretapped the offices of the Iraqi mission—with full legal authorization from the special federal court overseeing wiretaps—and overheard the Iraqi first secretary, Hamid Ahmed al-Amery, offer a former driver for the mission $50,000 to kill the Iraqi dissidents. One of them had headed an organization called Bet Nahrain, which had supported the restoration of political independence for Iraq's Assyrian minority. The driver agreed to carry out the assassination.

The plot was foiled by the FBI, even though they had a difficult time disentangling the conspiracy and had to first translate Assyrian and Arabic into English. Because of his diplomatic status, the Iraqi first secretary had immunity from arrest—but he was declared persona non grata and expelled from the country.

Jonathon Moil was a young British journalist who visited Chile in March 1990 to pursue a story on how Iraq had secretly purchased American helicopters through the Chilean arms company Cardoen. The American helicopters, manufactured by Bell, had been refitted by Cardoen with an advanced firing system. But Iraqi agents found out about Moil's investigation. According to Western intelligence, Baghdad ordered that Moil be eliminated. On March 29, 1990, Moil was found dead in his hotel room in Santiago. He had been beaten in his bed and then hanged.

In Baghdad, a month later, Iraqi agents executed another British subject, this time an employee of the British Matrix Churchill Company, which had supplied nuclear triggers to Iraq. Gordon Glass had worked in an SS-missile production plant—but he was put under surveillance by Iraqi intelligence after embarrassing leaks of the secret nuclear-trigger sale had appeared in the British and other Western press. Glass had been fingered by Iraqi

intelligence. On the evening of May 16, Glass was returning to his hotel in downtown Baghdad when half a dozen
men suddenly surrounded him. They began beating him
mercilessly. Glass staggered into his hotel room and was
found dead the next morning.

During the mid-1980s, Iraq carefully nurtured relations
with other regimes also actively involved in the promotion
of international terror. The most extensive of these was
established with East Germany; the two countries ex-
changed intelligence and trained each other's terrorist
forces to carry out attacks.

According to West German intelligence, the East German secret police, known as the Stasi, established a separate liaison office that coordinated joint projects with Iraqi
terrorists and military officials—from the development of
nerve gas to the training of urban terrorists. A de facto
exchange program between the two countries was set up.
East Germany, together with other Eastern bloc countries, sent military officers to Palestinian terrorist training
camps. Ivan Ilych Ramirez, better known as Carlos, spent
the better part of two years in Baghdad, according to
Israeli intelligence sources. Officers of the HVA, the for-
eign-espionage branch of the Stasi, worked on loan as
advisers to the Iraqi military. A special joint Stasi–East
German military detachment worked exclusively on helping the Iraqis develop delivery systems to project nerve gas
and safely transport biological weapons for attacks on
urban targets. Several Stasi officers were based at two
Palestinian terrorist-training camps in Al-Aziziya and Al-
Musayyib, which are within a hundred-mile radius of
Baghdad.

The Stasi routinely trained Baghdad-based Palestinian
terrorists, who were provided with diplomatic cover

through the Iraqi embassy in Berlin. At one point in 1986, according to West German and Israeli intelligence officials, there were more than fifty Iraqi-based Palestinian terrorists training in Stasi military camps and laboratories. The Stasi trained these terrorists in chemical warfare, use of explosives, demolitions, and cover and deception to infiltrate Israel and West European countries.

A former Stasi officer, interviewed in a January 1991 British television documentary, admitted that he trained Iraqi military operatives how to use chemical warfare in a twelve-thousand-acre Stasi military camp in Massow, south of Berlin. At the camp, the Stasi officer said, there was extra emphasis on targeting heavily populated civilian centers.

But Iraq did not limit its terrorist exchange program to Eastern bloc countries or organizations. The Irish Republican Army sent men to train in several terrorist camps outside Baghdad. According to Israeli intelligence reports, the IRA men ended up as instructors to Palestinian terrorists. The Japanese Red Army, the Baader-Meinhof, Red Army Faction, and the Italian Red Brigades also trained in Iraq and received false passports there to better disguise their travels in Europe.

But beginning in 1988, the Eastern bloc security services started to disintegrate under the weight of their own failing Communist societies. As a result, their ties to Iraq began to loosen dramatically—although Iraq contracted with nearly one hundred East German scientists and "former" Stasi officers to stay in Iraq and continue their work.

Still, in the absence of the support system provided by the Eastern bloc ties, Iraq found itself looking to replenish its stock of terrorist resources. Baghdad openly branched out to Palestinian terror groups once again, offering to provide money, weapons, and political support. Saddam Hussein became the Palestinians' godfather—in exchange for their support down the road.

In the fall of 1989, Abu Nidal's nephew opened an office for Nidal in downtown Baghdad. This marked Nidal's official return to Iraq after a six-year absence—an absence that had been repeatedly touted by State Department officials as evidence of Iraqi repudiation of terrorism. In fact, the Iraqi government had continued to fund Abu Nidal through transfers of millions of dollars to his Swiss bank accounts. It was both ideological and tactical. Because Nidal had moved his headquarters to Iraq's archenemy, Syria, in 1983, Iraq wanted to ensure that he would not turn his terror apparatus against the Iraqis. In December 1990, Nidal himself visited Baghdad, where an agreement to fight Israel and the West was officially inaugurated.

Ahmed Jabril, the head of the Popular Front for the Liberation of Palestine—General Command, soon followed in Nidal's footsteps. Jabril, who had carried out the bombing of Pan Am Flight 103 in December 1988, which blew up over Lockerbie, Scotland, and killed 270 people, was trying to diversify his pool of employers. Iraq offered to provide him with diplomatic passports and additional funds to be used to help "liberate Palestine from the Zionist enemy," according to intelligence reports received by the United States and Israel.

In the spring of 1990, the resurrection of the old terrorist coalition was nearly complete. Saddam Hussein gathered the heads of the top Palestinian terrorist clans, men who would normally be plotting each other's deaths. The historic meeting was not unlike the infamous meetings of Mafia family chieftains, who would get together in a morale-building reunion to remind each other of the common enemy—despite the fact that the members of their rival organizations were usually engaged in killing each other. This was an opportunity for Saddam Hussein to demonstrate that he was becoming the chief backer of the Palestinian cause—in return for which he expected the terrorist chiefs to make their extensive organizational infrastructures available for his use.

Attending the Baghdad meeting were some of the most notorious Palestinian terrorists in the world, men responsible for the deaths of *thousands* of people in bloody attacks over the previous twenty-five years. They included: Abu Abbas, head of the Palestine Liberation Front; George Habash, head of the Popular Front for the Liberation of Palestine; Nayaf Hawatmeh, head of the Democratic Front for the Liberation of Palestine; Samir Gousha, head of the Popular Struggle Front; Salim Abu Salem, head of the Popular Front for the Liberation of Palestine—Special Command. Even the aging master bomb maker himself, Abu Ibrahim, the man whose lethal technology had become disseminated throughout the terrorist movement, was on hand. Five new terrorist camps around Baghdad were opened in the three months following the historic meeting.

The head of the PLO, Yasser Arafat, did not show up. He apparently did not, at that time, want to jeopardize his ongoing dialogue with the United States. But his relationship with Hussein had already been solidified. In April 1990, Iraq provided $40 million to the PLO. The PLO chairman, according to American intelligence sources, gave his approval to the elaborate terror attack perpetrated by his colleague Abu Abbas on the Israeli coast in May 1990. The terrorists broke into two groups 170 miles off the Israeli coast, where they piloted two speedboats and headed for Tel Aviv. Israeli forces intercepted the terrorists before they could carry out their plans to kill hundreds of Israelis and to kill anyone they encountered in the American Embassy in Tel Aviv. Though the terrorists had left from a Libyan base, a still-secret Israeli interrogation of the captured men proved that Iraq had secretly assisted Abbas in carrying out the operation. One of the terrorists admitted that he had trained for forty days in a camp in Narayia near Baghdad, where he was taught how to use explosives. The ties between Abu Abbas—who still travels on the diplomatic passport given him by Iraq in 1985—and Baghdad have grown by leaps and bounds since he was given refuge in Iraq following the *Achille Lauro* hijacking.

After the unsuccessful attack on Israel, Abbas effectively became a hit man for Saddam Hussein. He repeatedly threatened to "attack American interests and targets" on behalf of Iraq. Only days after Iraq invaded Kuwait in August 1990, Abbas urged his forces to "open fire on the American enemy everywhere." Not insignificantly, Abbas's organization was prominently represented in the PLO.

Arafat's PLO forces already had been integrated into the Iraqi military. Under the stewardship of Iraq-based Haj Ismail, Fatah forces were organized in the Al-Aska division, which specialized in carrying out cross-border penetration terror attacks. In 1988, according to Western intelligence, there were eight hundred PLO terrorists training in Iraq who belonged to Arafat's Fatah branch. By the summer of 1990, there were an estimated eleven hundred PLO terrorists from the Fatah branch training in military camps in Iraq.

16

Saddam's Allies

This is being written in mid-March 1991. The American-led allied forces have emerged victorious over the Iraqi military. The devastation of the Iraqi armed forces is almost beyond belief—at least twenty-five thousand dead. Their military machine is annihilated. The United States has pulled off what can be considered one of the most impressive performances in modern military history—although the future will probably record the fact that the United States overestimated the power of the Iraqi army. Nevertheless, Iraq stands wasted, its weapons of mass destruction destroyed.

But the key question that no one seems to be asking is whether it had to happen this way.

On August 2, 1990, Iraq stunned the world with its ruthless and brazen invasion of Kuwait. It prompted an immediate military mobilization and deployment of American troops. But in fact, Saddam Hussein's belligerent intentions were manifestly clear by April 1990. In a fiery speech on Baghdad radio, he boasted of having acquired advanced chemical weapons. He threatened to burn half of Israel. Two weeks before, an Iraqi revolutionary court imposed a death sentence on Farzad Barzoft, an Iranian-born British journalist, for allegedly spying for Israel and Great Britain. Despite appeals for clemency from around the world, Barzoft was executed.

These acts, no matter how heinous, were minor compared to what had gone on in Iraq in previous years. The United States and the West had effectively closed their eyes and ears to the fact that for the previous decade, nearly every single governmental or private institution in Iraq was mobilized to acquire the basic components of a nuclear, biological, and chemical, and ballistics weapon development program designed for only one possible thing—mass terror.

Intelligence officials in the United States readily admit they had collected evidence that, to acquire these tools of mass destruction, Saddam Hussein's regime had set up scores of dummy organizations, front companies, and corporations that existed in letterhead only. Names such as the "Iraqi Trading Company," the "Saddam Hussein Organization," the "Iraqi Ex-Im Corporation," the "Iraqi Business Council," and the "Iraq Tourist Development Council." Iraq also funded research and development through other countries like Brazil and Egypt.

Of course, the sad truth was that Iraq didn't need to use subterfuge to expand and develop its arsenal of chemical, biological, and nuclear weapons; corporations and governments around the world eagerly sought to export weapons of mass destruction to them. In his master plan, Saddam Hussein had one very important—and all-too-willing—accomplice: the world. According to a classified CIA report prepared in 1990, ninety-two countries sold vital military equipment and sensitive technology to Iraq between 1983 and 1989. The countries made up a veritable United Nations, including nearly every Western and Soviet bloc country in the world. Voracious Iraq embarked on a massive spending spree: Between 1983 and 1990, it was the single largest purchaser of foreign weapons in the world.

The Soviet bloc, for example, sold Iraq tens of billions of dollars' worth of military weapons—Hind C helicopters, MiG-29 fighters, T-62 and T-72 tanks, air-to-air and air-to-surface missiles, Scud missiles, warships, minesweepers, armored personnel carriers. France sold Iraq armored personnel carriers and more than one hundred planes. Italy sold Iraq 115 helicopters and hundreds of missiles. *Even the United States sold Iraq thirty-one Model 241ST helicopters.*

More than one hundred German companies provided everything from combat helicopters, multiple rocket launching systems, chemical-proof underground bunkers, strains of deadly mycotoxins, ballistic missile technology, deadly enhancement of the Scud missile technology. The area where German corporations made their largest "contribution" was in transforming Iraq into the largest producer of poisonous gas and chemical weapons in the world. By 1990, Iraq was producing at least five thousand tons of chemical weapons a year.

The floodgates of American exports opened shortly after the United States and Iraq resumed diplomatic relations in 1984. The next year, more than three dozen American businesses were invited to display their wares in Iraq's business exhibition in Baghdad. That initiated a deluge of American companies trying to export to Iraq. The Export-Import Bank, an American agency that offers financial incentives to American exporters, provided Iraq with $250 million in credit beginning in 1986. Under another subsidized financial insurance program set up at the Department of Agriculture, the Commodity Credit Corporation began approving credits for Iraq to purchase American grain. In 1982, as pointed out in the book *Saddam Hussein and the Crisis in the Gulf* by Judith Miller and Laurie Mylroie, the U.S. provided $215 million in credits; by 1990, the figure had burgeoned to $1.045 billion. U.S.-Iraqi trade had risen to $3.6 billion. The Italian Banca Nazionale de Lavoro authorized $2.5 billion in loans to Iraq through its branch in Atlanta, Georgia.

The huge growth in the economic relationship between Iraq and the United States was in itself a self-propelling factor in ensuring that the Iraqi-U.S. relationship was shielded from any critical scrutiny. It spawned powerful vested and commercial interests in the United States who would protect and guarantee that this "special relationship" remained immune from tampering. High-powered lobbyists, such as Marshal Willey, former ambassador to Oman and a former chief of the U.S. mission in Baghdad, became head of the U.S.-Iraq Business Forum, an umbrella organization of American blue-chip corporations. The organization helped successfully weaken a sanctions bill against Iraq that had been proposed in Congress. It also lobbied in 1988 against a bill that would have restricted Iraqi trade after evidence surfaced that Iraq had gassed its Kurdish minority. In August 1990, two weeks after Iraq had invaded Kuwait, Willey was quoted in the *Los Angeles Times* as saying about Saddam Hussein, "We've focused a little too much on his brutal side. . . . In a personal meeting with him, he can be charming."

Others who lobbied for Iraqi interests included Richard
Fairbanks, a former Middle East special envoy in the
Reagan administration; Mary King, a former Carter administration official; James Placke, a former deputy assistant secretary of state for Near Eastern affairs. Former
Senator Charles Percy, who emerged as a propagandist for
Arab issues since his departure from the Senate, became
an active member of the U.S.-Iraq Business Forum. Organizations in Washington, such as the American Educa-
tional Trust, which publishes the *Washington Report on
Middle East Affairs,* received contributions directly and
indirectly from Iraq, the U.S.-Iraq Business Forum, Iraqi
businesses, and Iraqi front organizations. In turn, these
organizations and the people affiliated with them became
effective mouthpieces for Iraq, promoting Saddam Hussein and the notion that he and his regime were politically
moderate.

Economic largesse was bestowed by pro-Iraqi founda-
tions throughout the United States, providing expenses-
paid trips, honoraria, and fellowships to some of the
country's most prominent Middle East experts, to aca-
demic institutions, and to former government officials. In
Washington alone, Iraqi governmental entities, according
to a highly classified intelligence report assembled in early
1990, spent close to $10 million cultivating sympathy and
support among the Washington intelligentsia during the
previous five years.

One of the most questionable developments in American policy toward Iraq was the Commerce Department's
approval of nearly fifteen hundred export licenses worth
$1.5 billion to American companies seeking to sell "dual-
use" technology to the Iraqis. Because dual-use technology can be used for both civilian and military purposes,

approval must be granted by the government to ensure that it is used only for civilian projects. To gain permission to import this technology, Iraqi officials insisted in letters to their American partners that they planned only benign and peaceful purposes for the American items.

Yet it was unambiguously clear to American and Western intelligence officials and to senior officials in the Pentagon—such as Stephen Bryen who served as a deputy undersecretary at the Department of Defense during the Reagan administration—that there was conclusive evidence the Iraqis would be using the technology for explicit military projects. These officials' concerns were both ignored and overruled. As a result, the United States directly helped build up Saddam Hussein's monster regime.

Even after Iraq had invaded Kuwait and all U.S. trade with Iraq was banned, the Commerce Department refused to make the list of license applications public, citing "propietary" reasons. But because the contracts were no longer in effect, congressional critics dismissed the Commerce Department's explanation as a smokescreen for the real reasons: political embarrassment. And it is easy to see why.

At the Iraqi ballistic-missile complex at Saad 16, for example, as pointed out by Henry Weinstein and William C. Remple of the *Los Angeles Times*, "U.S. firms provided such products as advanced computers, electronic instruments, and high-grade graphic terminals for rocket testing and analysis; flight simulaters and test equipment; microwave communications gear; radar maintenance equipment and computer mapping systems."

With official U.S. approval and encouragement, American companies shipped directly to the Iraqi Atomic Energy Commission, the Iraqi air force, and the Iraqi Ministry of Defense.

MBB Helicopters, a German-based company, applied in February 1985 for an export license to sell VIP helicopters to the Iraqi air force. A month later, the Commerce Department approved the $9 million sale of the helicopters, which intelligence officials say has become part of Saddam Hussein's personal fleet. Another corporation received permission two years later to sell $8 million of helicopters to Iraq. The purchaser? The Iraqi Ministry of Defense. On the application, the corporation stated that the "helicopters will be used to transport passengers, supplies, as well as medical evacuation."

The Commerce Department did not even examine the applications of Iraqi purchasers that, by virtue of who they were, warranted automatic scrutiny.

McDonnell Douglas was authorized to sell $17 million of helicopters to the Ministry of Agriculture in 1985 for "agricultural spraying." When Iraqi gassed its Kurdish citizens, it used similar "agricultural spraying" helicopters—intelligence officials could not confirm the exact make of the helicopters used—and artillery shells to drop poison gas.

Zeta Labs was allowed to sell $1.1 million of quartz crystals to Salah-al-Din, an arm of the Iraqi ballistic-missile project. Hewlett Packard was given the go-ahead to sell synthesizers to Salah-al-Din that were explicitly to be used, according to the Commerce application, to help "calibrate and adjust" Iraqi radar systems.

The largest deal approved by the Commerce Department amounted to more than half a billion dollars for the sale of three thousand five-ton cargo trucks to Iraq. The application, submitted by a corporation called Gateway International, was filed at Commerce in April 1988. Less than ninety days later, Commerce officials approved the application. Though demonstration trucks were sent to Iraq in anticipation of the deal, the Iraqi invasion of Kuwait halted the commercial transaction.

According to the still-secret Commerce Department list, Iraqi Airways had been given approval to purchase more than $20 million in dual-use technology from American manufacturers. This was a curious decision because Iraqi Airways, according to American and German intelligence officials, had been used so often to transport bombs from Baghdad to other cities that the airline was cynically dubbed in certain American intelligence quarters the "official airline of Iraqi terrorists." From 1982 through 1989, terrorists were waved through security at Baghdad International Airport and allowed to bring explosives and weapons on board when travelling abroad. Even the State Department, in a special report on Iraqi terrorism distributed in November 1990, cited Iraqi Airways as an instrument to carrying out international terrorist attacks.

According to the license applications, the Commerce Department approved multiple sales of spare parts, helicopters, and computers to Iraqi Airways over the past five years. In one sale, Memphis International was allowed to sell $4.3 million worth of gyroscopes and compasses to Iraqi Airways in September 1987. The same year, the Iraqi Airways branch headquartered in the United States was given permission to sell $13 million worth of helicopters. Still another sale provided $5 million in high-tech computers to the airline.

In probably what is the most telling case of confused American policy, four days before the Iraqi invasion of

Kuwait—when U.S. intelligence had noted that Iraq had massed one hundred thousand troops on the Kuwaiti border and was poised for an immediate invasion—the U.S. Commerce Department gave approval to what turned out to be the final export license application for the sale of high-tech computers to Iraq. The purchaser? The Iraqi Ministry of Defense.

17

Winners and Sinners

Abu Ibrahim's legacy continues to haunt the West. The bomb that blew up Pan Am Flight 103 over Lockerbie, Scotland, in December 1988 and the one that destroyed the Union des Transports Aeriens airplane over Niger in April 1989 were both barometric bombs. A total of 441 people lost their lives in those two explosions. "These bombs came out of the technology of one man—Abu Ibrahim," said Billy Vincent, the former director of security for the FAA. Vincent is deeply perturbed by what has happened. "We have only ourselves to blame for the fact that his technology has metastasized like a cancer. Abu Ibrahim is the father of these bombs. Make no mistake— Iraq was his patron."

Right up to the American-led battle to liberate Kuwait, Ibrahim, safely living in Baghdad, continued to represent a threat to the United States. In an interview in December 1990, the FBI's chief counterterrorism official, Buck Revell, said, "Let us say that we have always considered Abu Ibrahim and his operatives a continuing threat."

For Buck Revell, Billy Vincent, Howard Teicher,

Denny Kline, Vince Cannistraro, Victoria Toensing, the late Don Fortier, William Gilman, and all the others over the years who had to contend with the tilt toward Iraq, the battle was ultimately a losing cause. Yes, Rashid had been caught and arrested, and that was not an insignificant victory against the source of terrorism. But the larger source, the Iraqi government, had continued to get away with what one official bitterly called a "joint State Department–Commerce Department approved license to kill."

On November 5, 1990, the State Department issued a "fact sheet" detailing "Iraq's Support for Terrorists." The three-page report warned ominously of Saddam Hussein's call for a *jihad* against American and Western interests. The report noted that "Iraq has a worldwide network available to support terrorist operations [including] civilian and military intelligence officers, diplomatic facilities, Iraqi Airways offices, and Iraqi cultural centers. . . ." Curiously—and outrageously—the report dealt with the period from 1980 through 1988 by disingenuously sweeping aside Iraqi support for terrorism: "Iraq's interest in terrorism against Western targets waned during the 1980–1988 war with Iran."

Not only was the statement completely untrue but the dire warnings about Iraq's elaborate terrorist infrastructure implied that Iraq had suddenly developed it overnight.

"The bottom line," says former CIA chief counterterrorist official Vince Cannistraro, "is that Iraq never stopped supporting terrorism. It is we who stopped looking for it."

In the end, it is not only the U.S. government that is at fault for ignoring the Iraqi threat. The responsibility for allowing Saddam Hussein to get away with murder lies with academicians, the hordes of "Middle East experts" in Washington, and the media, whose simplistic and trendy views on the Middle East helped keep everyone's attention focused on the Arab-Israeli dispute as if that were the only cause of the region's problems. In the two years before the invasion of Kuwait, the television networks collectively had run more than three hundred critical stories focusing on Israel. In contrast, fewer than thirty stories focused on Iraqi human-rights violations or its weapons of mass destruction. Not one story ever talked about Iraq's continuing support for terrorism. Evidence of such was willfully ignored. The net effect of this grotesque imbalance was to allow American policy to get away unscathed from any critical scrutiny by the media.

Judith Kipper, for example, a self-anointed "Middle East expert" used extensively by ABC News, has repeatedly elevated the Palestinian conflict in importance above all the other bitter internecine and even more intractable inter-Arab conflicts. In the days after the Iraqi invasion of Kuwait, Kipper confidently—and erroneously—predicted that Saddam Hussein would soon voluntarily withdraw his troops. On August 10, 1990, Kipper essentially endorsed the "linkage" that the Iraqi leader had championed, when she was quoted in the *Detroit Free Press* as saying: "If there were Palestinian-Israeli negotiations, you wouldn't have this anti-Americanism in the region. It might be impossible for Iraq to act this way." If there was one thing demonstrated by the Iraqi invasion of Kuwait and the subsequent bloodshed, it was that the Palestinian problem had absolutely *nothing* to do with what Saddam Hussein did.

In 1989 and 1990, syndicated columnists Rowland Evans and Robert Novak wrote no fewer than thirty columns condemning Israel, repeating over and over again the message that Israel was the chief source of conflict in the Middle East. Not one column was ever written about Iraq's use of terrorism or its acquisition of weapons of mass destruction. In fact, Evans and Novak actually wrote several columns attacking Saddam Hussein's critics for exaggerating Hussein's wrongdoings.

Even the venerable *Time Magazine* columnist and reporter Strobe Talbott felt so aggrieved by how Saddam Hussein was "demonized" as a modern-day Hitler in the weeks following his invasion of Kuwait that he felt compelled to write in *Time* (August 20, 1990) that it was really Israeli policies that were the cause of instability in the region. As a consequence, Talbott wrote, the "United States, as Israel's friend and guardian, will pay a price in its ability to deal with Arabs of all stripes, moderates as well as radicals." Nothing was farther from the truth, as events showed in January and February. (Talbott also charged that it was "particularly in Israel" where the Hitler analogy was made; in fact, it had come from the lips of President George Bush. Moreover, it was in Israel where the analogy was most deeply contested by those who lived under Hitler's rule and found the comparison offensive.)

On September 1, 1990, eight and a half years after the United States had taken Iraq off the list of countries supporting terrorism, the United States finally restored Iraq to the list. It had taken the conquest of another country to do it.

Epilogue

With the war over and Baghdad in ruins, Adnan doesn't know what has happened to his family. He remains glued to the television, waiting to see broadcasts of Iraq in the hope—albeit farfetched—that he might see their faces.

Mohammed Rashid is still in prison in Greece. The date of his trial keeps getting postponed—but American prosecutors are hopeful the trial will take place shortly. The whereabouts of Abu Ibrahim are not known.

Denny Kline has left the FBI. Vince Cannistraro has left the CIA. Victoria Toensing has left the Justice Department. Billy Vincent has left the FAA. Howard Teicher has left the National Security Council. Noel Koch has left the Department of Defense. A new group of investigators, prosecutors, intelligence analysts, and policymakers are now in charge.

As for Adnan, he isn't exactly sure.

Perhaps he's had eight names. Maybe nine. He's been relocated more than a dozen times since he walked into Baghdad International Airport with a tan garment bag slung over his shoulder.

The bomb sewn into its seams was never set off. The hundreds of people whose lives were in danger never knew it. The Noga Hilton still stands. Each day, guests stroll onto the deck and look out across Lake Geneva. They say you can see the Alps and Mont Blanc on the horizon.

And while Adnan, now forty-nine years old, realizes that he did the honorable thing by turning himself in to the American embassy eight and a half years ago in Bern, he still wonders. If he had the chance to do it all over again tomorrow, what would be his decision?

Just a few months ago Adnan hired a lawyer. It had never occurred to him that there was something that could be done to protect his civil liberties and acquire the possession most dear to him—an American passport.

The woes of one disenchanted would-be terrorist have been low priority. "I am tired of my life," Adnan says in his broken English. "I feel a hostage here."

In his years in the United States, Adnan, still a proud Palestinian, has developed new respect for his old adversaries the Israelis, and has come to see through the rhetoric and deception practiced by Arab governments.

He has seen how Israel has tried to put down the *intifada* and compares the lot of Palestinians in the occupied territories to that of those living in Arab countries. "Israel allows demonstrations—it allows anyone to talk to the press. But you won't find Palestinians demonstrating in Syria or Jordan or Libya—because they would be shot.

"My father always said he wished we had never left Palestine because he knew a lot of people who stayed and they had no problems. They still have their businesses and their homes. They may not agree with the politics but they are not treated badly—especially when you look at how we are treated in Arab countries."

Adnan is particularly bitter at the way Arab countries have used the Palestinians as pawns to distract the population from pressing problems at home. "These countries make saving Palestine their mission because they can build up their armies, keep their military dictatorships. But their armies are not there to fight Israel—they're there to keep their own people down and justify their own dictatorships."

And so, it has been a strange odyssey for Adnan Awad—from a refugee in Palestine to a member of a terrorist organization to a defector to the United States to a "star" witness for the United States. Asked whether it was worth it, Adnan will give you different answers on different days.

The biggest constant in his life is the daily reminder that he has still not obtained a passport, has still not become an American citizen. It is as if he isn't good enough.

"I've lost myself," he said. "I've lost myself. Who am I? I don't have a country, I don't have a name. If I had known it was going to take this long to help the Americans with their case and that, in the meanwhile, I would not be in control of my own life, I would never have come."

He once had thoughts of suicide. But instead of ending his life, Adnan has decided to just disobey the system that has made him so unhappy. Knowing that his life is in danger, he remains cautious, yet is unwilling to keep quiet. Though told not to, he insists on telling his story to the public. Keeping his mouth shut has not gotten him anywhere. "Ultimately nobody can protect my life," Adnan says. "Only God."

Without the FBI's official knowledge, Adnan lives with a striking, tall blond American woman in her mid-forties. She too has suffered. "Every time he walks out the door

I think, 'How long will I wait before I assume that he's never coming back again?' " she said. "Because at a moment's notice the government could whisk him away and that would be the end of it. It's a spooky way to live."

"Julia" has played an important role in Adnan's life, reading the mail that he cannot decipher, explaining the nuances of American culture to him, scrutinizing his television interviews before they air. "I'm always checking his shadow," she said. "Could his enemies recognize him?"

Dressed each day in a dishidashi, or customary Arabic clothes embroidered with 14-karat-gold thread, Julia is often stopped in the grocery store. One woman asked her where she gets her dresses.

"Damascus," Julia said.

"I've never heard of that store," the woman replied. "Is it new?"

Although Adnan and Julia will confirm only that they've known each other over the last three years, it seems as though they've been acquainted much longer. In a simple frame, an Arabic love poem from their courting days reads: *My eyes see your beautiful face between every line my pen writes. You are everything to me and each day my peace is broken because I am lonely and I almost lose my mind that I haven't seen you.*

They live together, with Julia's youngest son, in the last house on a dead-end street. The furnishings are modest. A menagerie of three Amazon lovebirds, two finches, three canaries, a pygmy goat, a kitten, and a snowy white Maltese named Mimi take the place of friends, which, up until Adnan decided to break his silence, they never were able to make.

Adnan spends his days working endlessly in his yard, fishing, and reclaiming a childhood talent—painting. His artwork is everywhere. Vigorous brush strokes in bright oils light up the corners of their home. Each canvas is signed in a different alias. The most striking is a landscape with a man running down the middle of the highway. Broken handcuffs dangle from his wrists, his arms triumphantly raised in the air.

Adnan does not nostalgically hold fast to many American dreams. They've mostly resulted in broken promises or unanswered prayers. But, with all his discontent, one wish has come true. He's the owner of a red 1966 Ambassador convertible. Every time he's been relocated, he's written a bill of sale to his new pseudonym.

"I never put a price on my information," Adnan says. "I'm not a whore. I made a decision to help the United States because of my honor. Nobody pressured me. I am not for sale. I just want to be treated with respect. I don't want to lie anymore. I want to put my name on a flag and wave it."

About the Authors

STEVEN A. EMERSON is a Washington-based correspondent specializing in national security issues. His reports appear regularly on CNN, and he frequently publishes in *The New York Times Magazine, The Wall Street Journal,* and *The New Republic.* The author of three other books, he is a three-time recipient of the Investigative Reporters and Editors Award for best national investigative reporting.

CRISTINA DEL SESTO is a Washington-based free-lance writer. She regularly contributes to *The Washington Post,* and her articles have also appeared in national magazines.